THE JOY OF

FROM HOT DOGS TO HAUTE CUISINE

BY BENNETT JACOBSTEIN

FOOD PHOTOGRAPHY BY
DEBORAH L. JACOBSTEIN

The Joy of Ballpark Food: From Hot Dogs to Haute Cuisine
Copyright © 2015 by Bennett Jacobstein

Published by Ballpark Food Publications
www.ballparkfood.org

ISBN 978-0-692-33654-0

Library of Congress Control Number: 2014922527
Ballpark Food Publications, San Jose, CA

Cover design and layout by Andy Nichols
Printed by Createspace

DISCLAIMER
All ballpark food photographs appearing herein, unless
otherwise noted, were taken by Deborah L. Jacobstein during
the 2014 Major League Baseball season. She was a paid
attendee along with the author, Bennett Jacobstein, and they
personally purchased the food products shown. Descriptions
are principally in the author's own words, except as otherwise
stated, and any errors are unintentional. Deborah L. Jacobstein
and Bennett Jacobstein are not affiliated with Major League
Baseball or any of the food purveyors at the ballparks.

To my father who took me to my first San Francisco Giants baseball game in 1965, and instilled in me a continuing love of baseball.

To my wife Debbie who finally became a baseball fan during the 2010 San Francisco Giants pennant race.

To my daughter Aviva and daughter-in-law Marya who have little interest in baseball, are vegetarian-inclined, but still were able to enjoy a Fenway Frank when I took them to a Red Sox game.

CONTENTS

ACKNOWLEDGMENTS

I would like to thank all my family and friends who encouraged me in this project.

Special acknowledgments:

to Tim Wiles and the staff of the Research Library at the National Baseball Hall of Fame for providing assistance and access to their collections.

to Fran Galt who used his extensive knowledge of both baseball and English grammar to edit the final text.

to N.E. for her assistance with research and helping me to get my thoughts down on paper.

to Ellen Gilmore for editing my initial drafts.

to Elizabeth, Kay, Gary, and the staff at the San Jose Giants concession stand who make being a ballpark vendor an incredibly fun experience.

to Mother Nature for allowing us to visit all 30 stadiums within one season without a rainout.

to Andy Nichols for providing the book layout and design.

to my wife Debbie for accompanying me to the stadiums, being my official food photographer, taste-testing foods that I didn't want to eat, and encouraging me when I needed it.

CELEBRATE THE JOY OF BALLPARK FOOD WHILE HELPING THOSE IN NEED OF FOOD

The goal of this book is to celebrate the joy of ballpark food while helping those in need of food. This book is independently published using the Createspace feature of *www.amazon.com*. All of the royalties from the sales of this book are being donated directly to the Second Harvest Food Bank of Santa Clara and San Mateo Counties of California.

Second Harvest Food Bank of Santa Clara and San Mateo Counties is the trusted leader dedicated to ending local hunger. Since its inception in 1974, Second Harvest has become one of the largest food banks in the nation, providing food to more than 250,000 people each month. The Food Bank mobilizes individuals, companies, and community partners to connect people to the nutritious food they need. More than half of the food distributed is fresh produce. Second Harvest also plays a leading role in promoting federal nutrition programs and educating families on how to make healthier food choices.

INTRODUCTION

According to the National Hot Dog and Sausage Council (yes, there really is such a thing), 21,357,316 hot dogs and 5,508,887 sausages are estimated to be consumed at major league ballparks in 2014. Clearly, the U.S. sporting public agrees with Charlie Brown that a baseball game in front of a hot dog makes the hot dog taste great.

Baseball is a game that is identified with food. We even sing about it at every ballpark during the seventh inning stretch: "....buy me some peanuts and Cracker Jack..." The famous song was written by Jack Norworth in 1908.

From the early part of the twentieth century until the 1980s, classic baseball fare consisted mostly of hot dogs, ice cream, peanuts, and Cracker Jack. Then ballparks slowly began to sell new items. Traditionalists fought against the expansion of the ballpark menu.

Now, teams around the country sell a variety of exotic food. To paraphrase Yogi Berra, if Jack Norworth were alive today, he'd be turning over in his grave to see Dungeness crab sandwiches on baguettes, smoked pastrami Reubens, garlic fries and veggie burgers now being sold at baseball stadiums.

Iconic movie actor Humphrey Bogart once said, "A hot dog at the ballgame beats roast beef at the Ritz." We go to the ballpark in order to put a baseball game in front of our hot dog (or today our Dungeness crab on a baguette).

In a 1988 best-selling book, author Bob Wood reports on his summer traveling to the then 26 major league baseball stadiums. Although the book mostly covered topics other than food, he chose to name it *Dodger Dogs to Fenway Franks: And All the Wieners in Between.* Food is indeed a defining factor for baseball fans.

The Joy of Ballpark Food: From Hot Dogs to Haute Cuisine begins with the history of the first hot dog at a ball game and concludes with a culinary tour of all 30 major league ballparks.

THE *Hot Dog* COMES TO AMERICA

Dreamland, Coney Island, N.Y., 1904. Library of Congress, LC-USZ62-115624.

Literary scholars have debated for decades whether Shakespeare actually wrote the plays attributed to him. Similarly, there are opposing theories, each with its own advocates, of how the hot dog as we know it came to be.

The familiar American hot dog is a type of German sausage served in a roll and handheld for eating. It is widely believed that many butchers in America commonly sold the sausage (known as a dachshund sausage) during the nineteenth century. What is in dispute, however, is who came up with the idea of putting the dachshund sausage in a roll or bun and calling it a hot dog.

Was it...

> … in the 1860s when a German immigrant whose name remains unknown sold them from a pushcart in New York City's Bowery?
>
> … in 1871 when Charles Feltman opened up a stand on Coney Island? (An employee of Feltman's, Nathan Handwerker, eventually went on to found Nathan's Famous Hot Dogs.)
>
> … in 1893 when they were introduced at the Chicago Columbian Exposition by Austrian immigrants Emil Reichel and Sam Ladany?
>
> … in 1893 when Chris Von de Ahe, St. Louis bar owner and owner of the St. Louis Browns baseball team, sold them at his ballpark?
>
> … in 1901 when Harry M. Stevens sold them at the Polo Grounds, home of the New York Giants, on a cold day when ice cream was not selling well? (More about this in the next chapter.)
>
> … in 1904 when a Bavarian sausage seller named Anton Feuchtwanger sold them at the St. Louis Louisiana Purchase Exposition? (As the story goes, he loaned white gloves to his customers to hold his hot sausages. Most of the gloves were not returned. He reportedly asked his brother-in-law, a baker, for help. The baker improvised long, soft rolls that fit the meat, thus inventing the hot dog bun.)

There are also reports of references to "hot dogs" appearing in college publications in the 1880s and 1890s.

As with the Shakespeare authorship dispute, the definitive answer to this mystery will probably never be known.

THE  COMES TO BASEBALL

A popular story states that at a New York Giants baseball game on a cold April day in 1901, pioneer vendor Harry M. Stevens was unable to sell ice cream. Instead he ordered his staff to purchase dachshund sausages from all the surrounding butcher shops. He then stuffed the sausages into bread rolls and shouted "Get your red hots!" Tad Dorgan, the sports cartoonist for the *New York Evening Journal*, was reputed to have been unable to spell *dachshund*, so he wrote *hot dogs* instead.

It is a wonderful story except for the fact that it is not true. Professor Gerald Cohen of the Missouri University of Science and Technology published a 293-page book entitled *Origin of the Term Hot Dog*. In the book Professor Cohen points out that, despite the widespread acceptance of this story, no copy of the cartoon has ever been found. Moreover, it appears that Dorgan was not even working for the *New York Evening Journal* in 1901.

Additionally, in an interview conducted by Fred Lieb of *The Sporting News* in 1926, Harry M. Stevens stated, "I have been given credit for introducing the hot dog in America. Well, I don't deserve it. It was my son Frank who first got the idea of selling hot dogs and wanted to try it on one of the early six-day bicycle race crowds at Madison Square Garden....At the time, we had been selling mostly sandwiches, and I told Frank that the bike fans preferred ham and cheese. He insisted that we try it out for a few days, and at last I consented. His insistence had all America eating hot dogs."

The cartoon myth probably would have died out if not for an article by Quentin Reynolds in *Colliers Magazine* in 1935. Harry M. Stevens had died in 1934 and Reynolds' article was a tribute to him. It is believed that Stevens' sons, out of loving memory to their father, did not object to Reynolds portraying the story as fact.

The first hot dog at a baseball game could have been at an 1893 St. Louis Browns (a member of the short-lived American Association baseball league) game, or could have been at a New York Giants game during the 1900s, or somewhere else.

What is clear, however, is that no one did more to popularize hot dogs and connect them to baseball than Harry M. Stevens.

"Hot Dogs" for Fans Waiting for Gates to Open at Ebbets Field, Oct. 6, 1920.
Library of Congress, LC-USZ62-58784.

Harry M. Stevens. National Baseball Hall of Fame Library, Cooperstown, NY.

Harry M. Stevens

Although we can't give Harry M. Stevens credit for inventing the hot dog, no one did more to connect hot dogs with baseball and to establish the connection between baseball and food.

In 1941, on the 50th anniversary of the founding of the Harry M. Stevens Catering Company, a celebratory dinner was held in New York. Harry M. Stevens' sons (Harry had passed away a few years earlier) received the following Western Union telegram:

"I have always known that there was more to your business than just selling hot dogs because a part of your fine personalities seemed to creep in to the flavor of the dogs. If my health permitted I would be with you tonight, but when I get going again, you will find me in the stadium rooting for McCarthy and the boys, with a season pass from Barrow in one hand and a Stevens hot dog in the other, and pride in my heart for all of you."

Lou Gehrig. National Baseball Hall of Fame Library, Cooperstown, NY.

The telegram was signed by Lou Gehrig.

The author of a newspaper column in the *El Paso Herald* in 1916 wanted to use a metaphor to indicate his subject's wealth. The metaphor he chose was "He has more money than Harry Stevens has hot dogs."

Harry Mosley Stevens was born in Litchurch (a village in Derbyshire), England, in either 1855 or 1856 (sources disagree). As a young man he immigrated to America and settled in Columbus, Ohio, where he obtained employment as a book salesman. Although Stevens is best known for his food empire, that was not his start in the baseball world.

Stevens attended baseball games of the Columbus Buckeyes in the Ohio State League. He was frustrated by the lack of information in the scorecards. There was very little discussion about the home team players and no mention at all of the visiting team players. Through his work as a book salesman, he had become acquainted with Ralph Lazarus, one of the owners of the Columbus Buckeyes. Lazarus sold Stevens the rights to produce and sell a new scorecard for the Buckeye games.

Stevens bought the scorecard rights for $500. By the next afternoon, he had sold $700 worth of advertising space in the scorecard. So before he even sold his first scorecard, he had already made a nice profit.

Legend has it that Harry came up with the slogan "You can't tell the players without a scorecard!" when he was peddling his scorecards in Columbus.

To call attention to the new scorecards, Stevens dressed in a red coat and straw hat. As he went through the grandstands with his scorecards, he recited lines from William Shakespeare and poet Lord Byron. Fans were able to have printed programs and lineup cards for the first time.

The scorecard was a success in Columbus, so Harry branched out first to Toledo and Milwaukee, and then to Pittsburgh, Cleveland, Washington, Boston, and Philadelphia.

Harry M. Stevens was always looking for new ways to expand his business. According to the September 2012 issue of *Columbus Monthly*, in 1887 Stevens opened the first food concession stand at a ballpark. This was at the Columbus minor league ballpark.

Stevens' big break came in 1894 when he obtained not only the scorecard rights for the New York Giants at the Polo Grounds but also the rights to food concessions in the ballpark. This would be the beginning of the Harry M. Stevens catering empire.

Before Harry M. Stevens came on the scene, what was sold at baseball games was mostly sandwiches, ice cream, and lemonade. By the turn of the twentieth century, these items had been replaced by hot dogs, peanuts, and soda pop. Stevens also was the concessionaire for horse races, bicycle races, and other New York area sporting events. In time Stevens branched out to providing food concessions at other major league baseball stadiums.

Harry M. Stevens died in 1934 in New York City. His obituary in the *New York Times* stated, "The thousands of uniformed men who proffer their wares, principally wieners, peanuts and pop, at all sorts of athletic contests in all parts of the country, owe their vocation to Mr. Stevens. He was the first of them and the most successful."

After his death the company, Harry M. Stevens, Inc., was taken over by his three sons and later by his grandsons and a fourth generation. In 1994, after over a hundred years in business, the company was bought by Aramark Sports and Entertainment Services.

Aramark is one of six companies (along with Delaware North Companies, Levy Restaurants, Center-plate, Legends, and Ovations Food Services) that now control the food concessions at all 30 major league baseball stadiums. In addition, they provide food services at many other stadiums and arenas.

New Polo Grounds, August 1911. Harry M. Stevens (left), John Foster, builder (center), John T. Brush, owner of New York Giants (right). National Baseball Hall of Fame Library, Cooperstown, NY.

What is a hot dog? And what is the difference between a hot dog and a sausage? These may seem like simple questions, but after spending an entire afternoon of Internet searching, I can assure you that they are not.

Since I began thinking about writing this book, I asked everyone I know (and some people I didn't know) what they thought the difference was between a hot dog and a sausage. Many answers I received reminded me of the famous quote from Supreme Court Justice Potter Stewart that "hard-core pornography" was hard to define but "I know it when I see it."

I asked this perplexing question to a crusty vendor with a hot dog and sausage cart on Yawkey Way outside of Fenway Park. His succinct response was to point to the hot dog and say "This is a hot dog" and point to the sausage and say "This is a sausage."

After searching through many sources, the best definition I have found is from the website *www. differencebetween.net* :

> 1. Sausage is an encompassing term for any processed meat with fat, spices, and preservatives that is encased into an animal's intestines or commercial wrapping. Many types of sausages are made and available in many markets; one of them is the popular American hot dog.

2. The hot dog is not an original sausage but merely an American adoption of German sausages, frankfurters, and wieners.

3. The texture of a hot dog is smooth and paste-like while sausages have a more composite mixture of miniscule bits of meat.

4. A hot dog is usually a food for leisure time while a sausage can be eaten for the same purpose and can also be used for main dishes.

According to food historian Bruce Kraig, author of *Hot Dog: A Global History*, "The hot dog species of sausage might be defined as an 'emulsified,' or very finely chopped or ground meat product. As a further subspecies, the hot dog is a precooked sausage. In its truly defined state, the hot dog is meant to be eaten out of the hand encased in a bun. In this sense, the hot dog crosses food categories and becomes one of America's singular foods, a sandwich."

Oftentimes children's book authors present concepts in a more cogent manner. Adrienne Sylver, the author of *Hot Diggity Dog: The History of the Hot Dog*, states "Hot dogs are a kind of sausage....The meats or veggies are chopped into small parts and blended with bread crumbs, flour, and seasonings. The gooey hot dog batter is pumped into a thin plastic tube to hold it together. Then it's cooked or smoked. Finally, the hot dog takes a bath in cool water and the plastic is peeled away."

And finally, for a clear and easy to understand definition, what better source to turn to than the United States *Code of Federal Regulations*:

> 9 CFR 319.180 - Frankfurter, frank, furter, hotdog, weiner, vienna, bologna, garlic bologna, knockwurst, and similar products.
>
> § 319.180
>
> Frankfurter, frank, furter, hotdog, weiner, vienna, bologna, garlic bologna, knockwurst, and similar products.
>
> (a) Frankfurter, frank, furter, hot-dog, wiener, vienna, bologna, garlic bologna, knockwurst and similar cooked sausages are comminuted, semi-solid sausages prepared from one or more kinds of raw skeletal muscle meat or raw skeletal muscle meat and raw or cooked poultry meat, and seasoned and cured, using one or more of the curing agents in accordance with a regulation permitting that use in this subchapter or in 9 CFR Chapter III, Subchapter E, or in 21 CFR Chapter I, Subchapter A or Subchapter B. They may or may not be smoked. The finished products shall not contain more than 30 percent fat. Water or ice, or both, may be used to facilitate chopping or mixing or to dissolve the curing ingredients but the sausage shall contain no more than 40 percent of a combination of fat and added water. These sausage products may contain only phosphates approved under part 318 of this chapter. Such products may contain raw or cooked poultry meat and/or Mechanically Separated (Kind of Poultry) without skin and without kidneys and sex glands used in accordance with § 381.174, not in excess of 15 percent of the total ingredients, excluding water, in the sausage, and Mechanically Separated (Species) used in accordance with § 319.6. Such poultry meat ingredients shall be designated in the ingredient

statement on the label of such sausage in accordance with the provisions of § 381.118 of this chapter.

(b) Frankfurter, frank, furter, hot-dog, wiener, vienna, bologna, garlic bologna, knockwurst and similar cooked sausages that are labeled with the phrase "with byproducts" or "with variety meats" in the product name are comminuted, semisolid sausages consisting of not less than 15 percent of one or more kinds of raw skeletal muscle meat with raw meat byproducts, or not less than 15 percent of one or more kinds of raw skeletal muscle meat with raw meat byproducts and raw or cooked poultry products; and seasoned and cured, using one or more of the curing ingredients in accordance with a regulation permitting that use in this subchapter or in 9 CFR Chapter III, Subchapter E, or in 21 CFR Chapter I, Subchapter A or Subchapter B. They may or may not be smoked. Partially defatted pork fatty tissue or partially defatted beef fatty tissue, or a combination of both, may be used in an amount not exceeding 15 percent of the meat and meat byproducts or meat, meat byproducts, and poultry products ingredients. The finished products shall not contain more than 30 percent fat. Water or ice, or both, may be used to facilitate chopping or mixing to dissolve the curing and seasoning ingredients, the sausage shall contain no more than 40 percent of a combination of fat and added water. These sausage products may contain only phosphates approved under part 318 of this chapter. These sausage products may contain poultry products and/or Mechanically Separated (Kind of Poultry) used in accordance with § 381.174, individually or in combination, not in excess of 15 percent of the total ingredients, excluding water, in the sausage, and may contain Mechanically Separated (Species) used in accordance with § 319.6. Such poultry products shall not contain kidneys or sex glands. The amount of poultry skin present in the sausage must not exceed the natural proportion of skin present on the whole carcass of the kind of poultry used in the sausage, as specified in § 381.117(d) of this chapter. The poultry products used in the sausage shall be designated in the ingredient statement on the label of such sausage in accordance with the provisions of § 381.118 of this chapter. Meat byproducts used in the sausage shall be designated individually in the ingredient statement on the label for such sausage in accordance with § 317.2 of this chapter.

(c) A cooked sausage as defined in paragraph (a) of this section shall be labeled by its generic name, e.g., frankfurter, frank, furter, hotdog, wiener, vienna, bologna, garlic bologna, or knockwurst. When such sausage products are prepared with meat from a single species of cattle, sheep, swine, or goats they shall be labeled with the term designating the particular species in conjunction with the generic name, e.g., "Beef Frankfurter," and when such sausage products are prepared in part with Mechanically Separated (Species) in accordance with § 319.6, they shall be labeled in accordance with § 317.2(j)(13) of this subchapter.

(d) A cooked sausage as defined in paragraph (b) of this section shall be labeled by its generic name, e.g., frankfurter, frank, furter, hotdog, wiener, vienna, bologna, garlic bologna, or knockwurst, in conjunction with the phrase "with byproducts" or "with variety meats" with such supplemental phrase shown in a prominent manner directly contiguous to the generic name and in the same color on an identical background.

(e) Binders and extenders as provided in § 319.140 of this part may be used in cooked sausage that otherwise comply with paragraph (a) or (b) of this section. When any such substance is added to these products, the substance shall be declared in the ingredients statement by its common or usual name in order of predominance.

(f) Cooked sausages shall not be labeled with terms such as "All Meat" or "All (Species)," or otherwise to indicate they do not contain nonmeat ingredients or are prepared only from meat.

(g) For the purposes of this section: Poultry meat means deboned chicken meat or turkey meat, or both, without skin or added fat; poultry products mean chicken or turkey, or chicken meat or turkey meat as defined in § 381.118 of this chapter, or poultry byproducts as defined in § 381.1 of this chapter; and meat byproducts (or variety meats), mean pork stomachs or snouts; beef, veal, lamb, or goat tripe; beef, veal, lamb, goat, or pork hearts, tongues, fat, lips, weasands, and spleens; and partially defatted pork fatty tissue, or partially defatted beef fatty tissue.

[38 FR 14742, June 5, 1973]

TAKE ME OUT TO THE

"Take Me Out to the Ball Game" is the third most frequently played song in America (after "Happy Birthday" and "The Star-Spangled Banner") according to Tim Wiles, formerly of the National Baseball Hall of Fame and co-author of *Baseball's Greatest Hit: The Story of Take Me Out to the Ball Game.*

And what is the first thing ball game fans want to do when they get to the ballpark? "Buy me some peanuts and Cracker Jack."

This American classic song was written by Jack Norworth in 1908 with music composed by Albert Von Tilzer. Norworth had written many popular songs including "Shine on Harvest Moon." Von Tilzer also founded a publishing company and was the first to publish compositions by both Irving Berlin and George Gershwin. Although both Norworth and Von Tilzer have strong credentials in the field of music, neither of them knew anything about baseball at the time the song was written.

Norworth was riding on the New York subway when he got the idea for the song lyrics from a sign advertising a baseball game at the Polo Grounds. Von Tilzer matched the lyrics to a tune he had previously composed. Neither of them had ever attended a baseball game. They were spot on about the peanuts and Cracker Jack. Harry M. Stevens had been selling peanuts at baseball games for years. And Cracker Jack was first sold at a ballpark in 1896. It would be 32 years before Norworth attended his first baseball game. Unfortunately, we have no record of what he had to eat.

Norworth was married for a time to singer-actress Nora Bayes. Together they were a well-known celebrity couple of the day. Nora was the first to sing "Take Me Out to the Ball Game." Others followed, and the song became popular in vaudeville shows and at intermissions in movie theaters -- but not yet at baseball games.

The first time "Take Me Out to the Ball Game" was sung at a baseball game was in 1934 at a Los Angeles high school game. The first time it was played at a major league game was the performance of the St. Louis Cardinals band led by third baseman Pepper Martin before game four of the 1934 World Series.

It is unclear when "Take Me Out to the Ball Game" was first sung during the seventh inning stretch, as is now the tradition. Although it was sung at some stadiums prior to the 1970s, legendary broadcaster Harry Caray popularized the song by singing it first to the crowds at the Chicago White Sox games during the 1970s, and later at the Chicago Cubs games.

The lyrics that we sing during the seventh inning stretch are actually the chorus of the song. The verses of the song tell the story of a girl who prefers to be taken to a ball game rather than a show.

Jack Norworth at the Piano. National Baseball Hall of Fame, Cooperstown, NY.

Changes were made to the lyrics in 1927 but the chorus that we all know was not changed. The most famous line of the song remains "Buy me some peanuts and Cracker Jack."

1908 version:

Katie Casey was baseball mad.
Had the fever and had it bad;
Just to root for the home town crew,
Ev'ry sou Katie blew.
On a Saturday, her young beau
Called to see if she'd like to go,
To see a show but Miss Kate said,
"No, I'll tell you what you can do."

Chorus

"Take me out to the ball game,
Take me out with the crowd.
Buy me some peanuts and Cracker Jack,
I don't care if I never get back,
Let me root, root, root for the home team,
If they don't win it's a shame.
For it's one, two, three strikes, you're out,
At the old ball game."

Katie Casey saw all the games,
Knew the players by their first names;
Told the umpire he was wrong,
All along good and strong.
When the score was just two to two,
Katie Casey knew what to do,
Just to cheer up the boys she knew,
She made the gang sing this song:

Chorus

"Take me out to the ball game,
Take me out with the crowd.
Buy me some peanuts and Cracker Jack,
I don't care if I never get back,
Let me root, root, root for the home team,
If they don't win it's a shame.
For it's one, two, three strikes, you're out,
At the old ball game."

1927 version:

Nelly Kelly loved baseball games,
Knew the players, knew all their names,
You could see her there ev'ry day,
Shout "Hurray," when they'd play.
Her boy friend by the name of Joe
Said, "To Coney Isle, dear, let's go,"
Then Nelly started to fret and pout,
And to him I heard her shout.

Chorus

"Take me out to the ball game,
Take me out with the crowd.
Buy me some peanuts and Cracker Jack,
I don't care if I never get back,
Let me root, root, root for the home team,
If they don't win it's a shame.
For it's one, two, three strikes, you're out,
At the old ball game."

Nelly Kelly was sure some fan,
She would root just like any man,
Told the umpire he was wrong,
All along, good and strong.
When the score was just two to two,
Nelly Kelly knew what to do,
Just to cheer up the boys she knew,
She made the gang sing this song.

Chorus

"Take me out to the ball game,
Take me out with the crowd.
Buy me some peanuts and Cracker Jack,
I don't care if I never get back,
Let me root, root, root for the home team,
If they don't win it's a shame.
For it's one, two, three strikes, you're out,
At the old ball game."

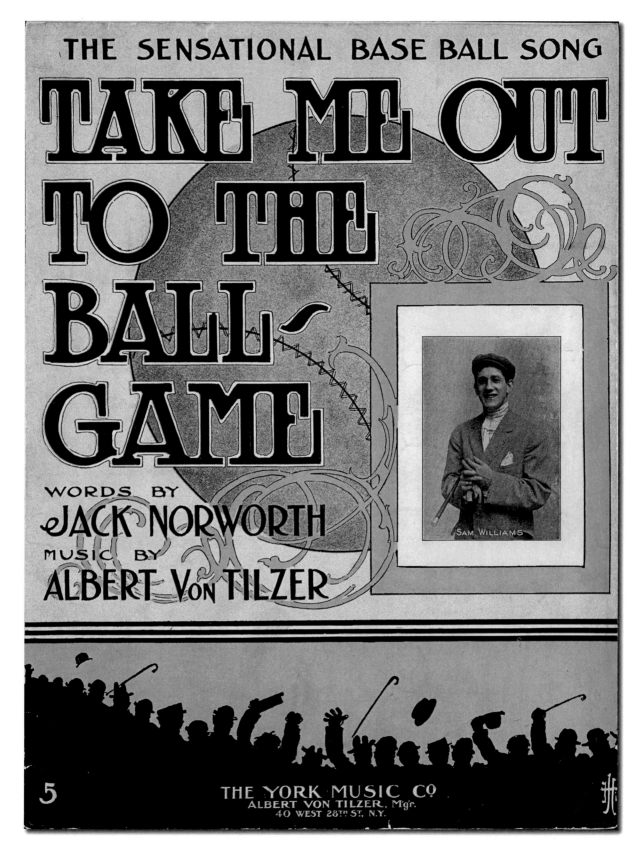

Take Me Out to the Ball Game, 1908.
Library of Congress Baseball Sheet Music, 200033481.

Along with hot dogs and peanuts, Cracker Jack® popcorn is one of the early and traditional baseball foods. Although its famous connection with baseball through the song "Take Me Out to the Ball Game" did not occur until 1908, an 1896 scorecard for a game played in Atlantic City, New Jersey, between the Atlantic City Baseball Club and the Cuban Giants contained a Cracker Jack advertisement.

Frederick Rueckheim immigrated to Chicago from Germany in 1871. Frederick and his brother Louis sold popcorn from a cart in the streets of Chicago. Later they added a caramel coating and peanuts to create the popcorn candy which eventually was marketed as Cracker Jack.

It has been variously reported that the Rueckheims distributed their new product at the 1893 Chicago Columbian Exposition. There is no record of the brothers having a stand at the Expo, but it is possible that they hawked their product on foot throughout the fair.

In the nineteenth century "crackerjack" was a slang expression that meant "something very pleasing or

Cracker Jack Popcorn.
Courtesy of Frito-Lay North America Inc.

excellent." The story goes that a customer, upon tasting the pop corn concoction, exclaimed "That's crackerjack!" and the Rueckheims took that as the trade name. The Cracker Jack brand name was registered in 1896.

In 1912 toy surprises were first put into every Cracker Jack box. In 1914 and 1915 a baseball card was placed in each Cracker Jack box. Customers were unhappy because there was less space for the caramel corn, and the baseball card distribution was soon discontinued. However, a 1915 Ty Cobb card from a Cracker Jack box sold in 2005 for $94,709.

Each box of Cracker Jack has a picture of Sailor Jack and his dog Bingo. Sailor Jack was modeled after Robert Rueckheim, an eight-year-old nephew or grandson of Frederick (sources vary). Tragically, Robert died of pneumonia shortly after his image first appeared.

Cracker Jack remained a family business until it was sold to Borden Inc. in 1964. In 1997 ownership of the brand was transferred to Frito-Lay North America, Inc.

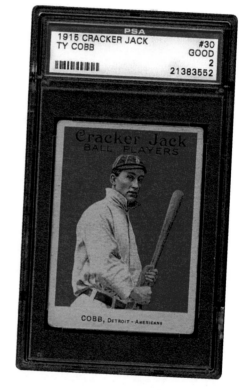

During the 1980s the New York Yankees hosted an Old-timers Game which was sponsored by the Cracker Jack brand. As part of the festivities, Cracker Jack was cooked on site for players and officials. According to game promoter Marty Appel, "The scent of hot Cracker Jack was almost indescribably wonderful. I'll always associate Cracker Jack with baseball, and the smell of hot Cracker Jack with the fun of those old-timers games."

In 2004 the New York Yankees decided to stop selling Cracker Jack and chose instead to offer another brand of caramel corn called Crunch 'n Munch. The decision left fans stunned and upset. Several months later, the Yankees corrected their error and brought back Cracker Jack. The Yankees' chief operating officer, Lonn Trost, gave the reason for the return of Cracker Jack: "The fans have spoken." Cracker Jack is currently sold at almost all of the major league stadiums.

1915 Cracker Jack Popcorn Ty Cobb Baseball Card.
Courtesy of Love of the Game Auctions.

Much credit for the popularity of Cracker Jack at baseball games can be given to "Take Me Out to the Ball Game." During the seventh inning of every baseball game across the country, fans are reminded of Cracker Jack. Although the Cracker Jack brand owes much of its success to the song, there is no evidence that songwriter Jack Norworth was ever compensated by the Rueckheims. Norworth was simply looking for a rhyme. If "back" did not rhyme with "jack," who knows what kind of snack baseball fans would be eating today.

Peanuts

Just as with the hot dog, Harry M. Stevens has a prominent role in the association of peanuts with baseball games. In 1895 the Cavagnaros peanut company wished to place an advertisement in one of Harry M. Stevens' scorecards but did not have money to pay for the ad. Instead Stevens offered to take payment in the form of peanuts, which he then sold at the stadium. According to *Amusement Business* magazine, this was the origin of the phrase "working for peanuts."

Hampton Farms Major League Baseball Peanuts Bags
Courtesy of Hampton Farms.

Peanuts became an instant success at baseball stadiums, and by the turn of the century they were standard ballpark fare along with hot dogs, popcorn, and Cracker Jack. Because of the increasing popularity of ballpark peanuts, Stevens later purchased land in Virginia and had peanuts grown for him there. He brought them to all his ballparks in truckloads.

About the same time that Stevens began to sell peanuts, three brothers, Marvin, Charles, and Louis Jacobs, were selling peanuts at Coney Island in New York. The brothers then moved to Buffalo, New York, and began selling peanuts at the local ballpark. In the early twentieth century they expanded to other ballparks that were not being served by Harry M. Stevens. In 1915 the brothers founded a company called Delaware North.

Delaware North Companies is now one of the six major companies that provide food concessions to the 30 major league baseball stadiums.

According to the *Washington Star*, Homer Rose (grandson of Harry M. Stevens), discussing peanuts, said "They've never been popular at race tracks because people need to keep their hands free for betting. In baseball, the tension builds slowly. Eating peanuts is part of the nervous habit -- it gives you something to do with your hands."

During the 1934 season, pitching stars Dizzy and Daffy Dean won 49 games between them for the world-champion St. Louis Cardinals. That same season their older brother Elmer was "pitching" bags of peanuts to customers in the stands at the Houston Buffaloes minor league park.

The off-Broadway musical *Diamonds,* directed by Broadway legend Harold Prince, made its debut in 1984. The show featured two characters: a child who wants to be a star slugger, and a peanut vendor in the stands. Although the show was not a commercial hit, this is yet another example of the importance of peanuts in baseball culture.

After retiring, many major league players have second careers relating to baseball. Hall-of-Fame pitchers Jim "Catfish" Hunter and Gaylord Perry chose a different career. They both became peanut farmers.

Hampton Farms is one of the leading retailers of peanuts. In grocery stores throughout the country, they are now selling "Major League Baseball" peanuts personalized with the logo of nearby major league teams. According to the Hampton Farms website, "Summer just wouldn't be the same without baseball and roasted in-shell peanuts. This classic combination has been delighting fans for generations, so it seemed only natural to combine America's favorite peanuts with America's favorite summer game."

However, eating peanuts is not an option for many ballpark fans. The Asthma and Allergy Foundation of America reports that approximately 2% of the U.S. population is allergic to peanuts. On June 29, 2013, the Chicago White Sox hosted an Allergy Awareness Day featuring nut-free seating sections. Brooks Boyer, White Sox Senior Vice President of Sales and Marketing, said: "Hopefully some of our fans and families who typically could not attend a White Sox game due to potential allergic reactions will be able to enjoy an

Jim "Catfish" Hunter. National Baseball Hall of Fame Library, Cooperstown, NY.

afternoon of White Sox baseball at U.S. Cellular Field." Likewise, the Baltimore Orioles have a "peanut allergy suite" available at reduced prices for those who need it. Similar considerations are catching on at other major and minor league parks.

I have been happily married for over 30 years and my wife and I seldom disagree about anything. A major disagreement we have, however, occurs when we go to a baseball game together and I purchase a bag of peanuts. I believe it is part of the great baseball tradition to throw your peanut shells on the floor. She believes this is rude and insists that I put my peanut shells in a bag and carry them out to the garbage can. Judging from the accumulation of peanut shells on stadium floors after the crowds file out, it seems that most people agree with me.

Peanuts were popular at ballparks before the song "Take Me Out to the Ball Game" became a standard, but having them mentioned at every seventh inning stretch certainly doesn't hurt sales.

FOOD OFFERINGS AND PRICES

During the course of my research at the National Baseball Hall of Fame Library, I was pleased to come across pictures of old-time scorecards and programs that included food listings and prices, as well as advertisements and other information. I have included the following nine examples spanning the years from 1937 through 1974.   Poring over these pictures is like looking through a window into our national past.

It is interesting to compare the prices for similar items that you can find at today's ballparks. In the 1930s a hot dog cost 10 cents; by 1974 it was 50 cents. Peanuts increased from 10 cents in 1937 to 30 cents in 1974.

In the 1938 program, directions to the "retiring rooms" for women say that there is a "matron always in attendance" -- a practice that has disappeared today.

Some surprising food offerings include filet of sole for 40 cents in 1952 from the Cincinnati Reds and a peanut butter sandwich for 10 cents in 1954 from the Orioles.

PHILADELPHIA ATHLETICS, 1937

Philadelphia Athletics Program. National Baseball
Hall of Fame Library, Cooperstown, NY.

BOSTON BRAVES, 1938

Boston Braves Scorecard. National Baseball Hall of
Fame Library, Cooperstown, NY.

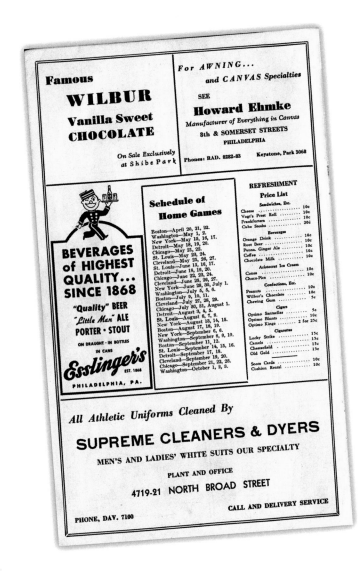

Rapid Transit—elevated and subway—Lines are the fast, direct route to the gates of Wrigley Field.

Ride **Howard Street-Jackson Park express trains** through the subway, or **Wilson Avenue local trains** over the elevated structure, to Addison Street station.

Subway transfers for west side "L" riders are issued at State-Van Buren station on the Loop elevated structure.

RAPID TRANSIT LINES
Elevated and Subway

Lunch Well — and Economically

You'll enjoy a snack at Wrigley Field, where we serve only the best of food and drinks, and at prices lower than you'll pay elsewhere. Pay no more than these listed prices.

Spicy Red Hots (Oscar Mayer's) . 15c	Pure Lemonade 20c
Juicy Ham Sandwiches 30c	Baby Ruth and other popular
Cheese Sandwiches 25c	candy bars 5c
Egg Sandwiches 20c	Chewing Gum 5c
Big Wedge of Pie 15c	Popcorn and Peanuts 10c
Borden's Ice Cream 10c	Camels, Chesterfields and other
Home-Brewed Coffee 10c	popular brands of cigarettes . . 20c
Borden's Milk and Buttermilk . . 10c	Wrigley Field Program 10c
Beer (Pabst) 25c	Pencils 5c
Coca Cola; Manhattan Orange and	Cushions (Rented) 10c
Root Beer; Orange Crush . . . 10c	Miniature Bats 50c

For all the news about the Cubs, listen to the Cub News of the Air over Radio Station WIND, at 7:30 every night, Monday through Saturday.

CHICAGO CUBS, 1947

Chicago Cubs Program. National Baseball Hall of Fame Library, Cooperstown, NY.

PITTSBURGH PIRATES, 1948

Pittsburgh Pirates Scorecard. National Baseball Hall of Fame Library, Cooperstown, NY.

CLEVELAND INDIANS, 1951

Cleveland Indians Scorecard. National Baseball Hall of Fame Library, Cooperstown, NY.

CINCINNATI REDS, 1952

Cincinnati Reds Scorecard. National Baseball Hall of Fame Library, Cooperstown, NY.

BALTIMORE ORIOLES, 1954

Baltimore Orioles Scorecard. National Baseball Hall of Fame Library, Cooperstown, NY.

PHILADELPHIA PHILLIES, 1967

Philadelphia Phillies Scorecard. National Baseball
Hall of Fame Library, Cooperstown, NY.

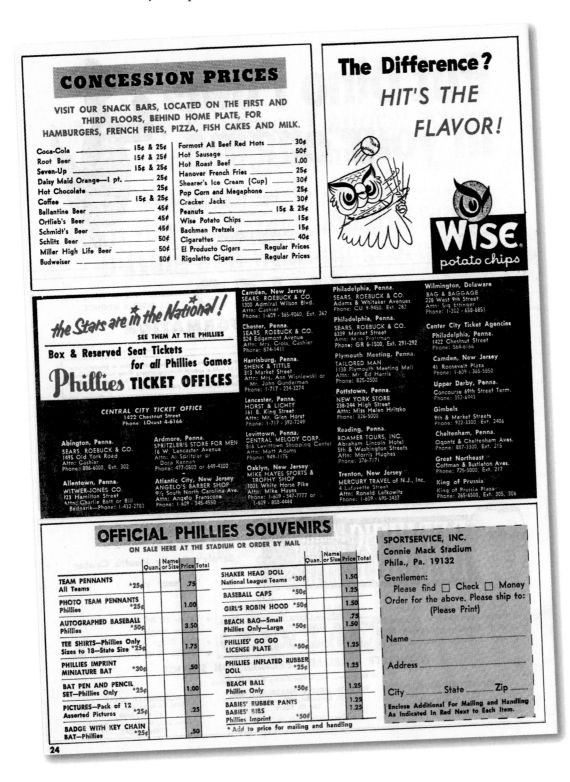

MINNESOTA TWINS, 1974

Minnesota Twins Program. National Baseball Hall of Fame Library, Cooperstown, NY.

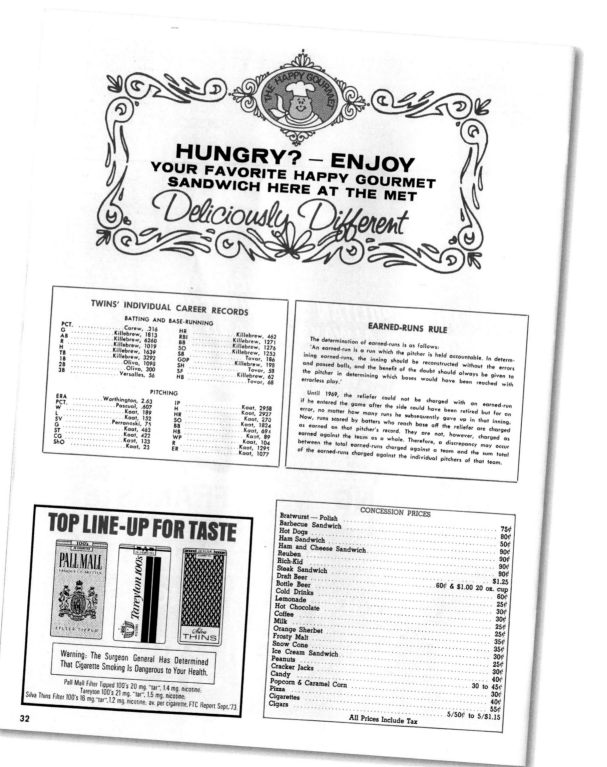

THE START OF THE

New Food Era

The traditional ballpark food consisting of hot dogs, peanuts, popcorn, and Cracker Jack did not change much from the late nineteenth century through the 1970s. During the 1980s new foods gradually began to be introduced. However, there was a proliferation of food offerings during the 1990s fueled by the opening of twelve new major league ballparks.

In the 1980s ballparks gradually began to expand their food offerings to include regional specialties. In 1982 food editor and author Elaine Corn wrote an extensive feature in the *Louisville Courier -Journal* entitled "Fans Fare: Expanding the Classics of Baseball." "Now, instead of simply the usual, fans can choose from a wide selection of regional delicacies from Boston to Hawaii. Fans have been stuffing themselves with Bratwurst at Bloomington, Minnesota, kosher products at New York's Shea Stadium, fried chicken at Pittsburgh, and manapua (a meat-filled or bean-paste-filled bun) in Honolulu."

Chicago-Style Pizza at Wrigley Field, Chicago, IL.

For the start of the 1988 season, the New York Yankees dramatically increased their food-choice concessions. They spent 2.5 million dollars during the winter to renovate the food stands and revitalize the menus. Their new menu items included pizza, roast

Grilled Wild Alaskan Salmon Sandwich at Safeco Field, Seattle, WA.

beef and pastrami sandwiches, egg rolls, shrimp, chicken fingers, hamburgers, and French fries. According to Craig S. Trimble, Vice President for Volume Services (now Centerplate), "...We have no intention of challenging the supremacy of the hot dog....We're just trying to add a little variety."

In a 1988 *New York Times* article entitled "New Yankee Call: Getcha Fresh Shrimp," it was reported that fan reaction was mixed. Yankee fan Robert Brown, while biting into a hot dog, asked, "Why would I come to Yankee Stadium and have a pastrami sandwich? If I wanted a pastrami sandwich, I'd go to a deli." Season ticket holder Martin Boeck said, "This roast beef is tender and delicious.... usually when you go to a stadium you get garbage....it seems like you're in the World's Fair." As it turned out, there are far more Martin Boecks than Robert Browns at the ballparks.

Between 1990 and 2000, twelve new major league ballparks were built. Rather than having to redesign the food stands as the Yankees had done in 1988, the new ballparks offered the opportunity to have optimally designed spaces for concession stands.

Tropicana Field in Tampa Bay offers Cuban sandwiches. Coors Field in Colorado has Rocky Mountain oysters. Wrigley Field in Chicago features Chicago-style pizza. Minute Maid Park in Houston has the famous Texas barbeque brisket. Safeco Field in Seattle has a grilled wild Alaskan salmon sandwich.

Oriole Park at Camden Yards in Baltimore and AT&T Park in San Francisco are among several ballparks that feature concessions stands owned by famous retired players from those teams. Former Oriole first baseman and 1970 American League Most Valuable Player Boog Powell owns Boog's Corner BBQ. Former San Francisco Giant and Hall of Famer Orlando Cepeda owns Orlando's Caribbean BBQ, featuring its Cha Cha bowl (jerk chicken, beans and rice).

By the end of the twentieth century, all ballparks were featuring a wide variety of food options, well beyond the wildest dreams of Harry M. Stevens.

Nachos AND Garlic Fries

In 1900 the most common snack foods served at ballparks were peanuts and Cracker Jack. By the end of the twentieth century, they had been supplanted by nachos and garlic fries.

Nachos were invented in 1943 by head waiter Ignacio "Nacho" Anaya in Piedras Negras, Coahuila, Mexico. One day after his restaurant (Victory Club) had closed and the chef had gone home, a group of women arrived. They were wives of U.S. soldiers stationed at Fort Duncan in nearby Eagle Pass, Texas. Wanting to serve them quickly, Anaya used what he had on hand – tortillas, cheese, and sliced jalapeños. After cutting the tortillas into small triangles, he covered them with shredded cheddar cheese and heated them so that the cheese melted and then topped them with the sliced jalapeños.

When asked what the dish was called, he replied "Nacho's Especiales," i.e., a specialty of Ignacio "Nacho" Anaya.

Pulled Pork Nachos at Progressive Field, Cleveland, OH.

The popularity of the dish spread quickly throughout Texas and the Southwest. In 1959 nachos were introduced at the El Cholo Mexican restaurant in Los Angeles.

Nachos could be found only at Mexican restaurants until 1973, when they were brought to the old Arlington Stadium, home of the Texas Rangers. According to Carey Risinger, Director of Food, Beverage and Retail at Arlington Stadium, "The standard concessions stand in the 70s was simple. We sold the basics: hot dogs, peanuts, and popcorn." Risinger wanted to add something new so he decided to open a nachos stand at the ballpark. To make the nachos, Cheez Whiz was melted in a hot fudge warmer and the mixture was ladled over circular corn chips. To help with consistency, jalapeño juice was added to the Cheez Whiz mix. The rest is history, and nachos are now sold at almost every sporting event throughout the country.

Garlic fries were created by Dan Gordon, one of the founders of Gordon Biersch Brewery Restaurants, while he was studying beer making at the Technical University in Munich, Germany. At the request of a professor, he spent a day doing research in a garlic field. At the end of the day he was served a meal featuring ten different dishes made with garlic. He was so inspired by the experience that he created the garlic and deep-fried potato combination as a late-night snack during his final exams.

Gordon Biersch Garlic Fries at AT&T Park, San Francisco, CA.

Garlic fries were first sold at the Gordon Biersch Brewery Restaurant in Palo Alto, California, in 1988. Gordon referred to them as "the perfect carb partner for our beers."

Garlic fries made their way into a ballpark in 1994 when Gordon Biersch opened a concession stand at Candlestick Park, former home of the San Francisco Giants. Garlic fries have now become a staple at almost all ballparks. At AT&T Park in San Francisco you don't have to worry about offending your seatmates with garlic breath, since each order of garlic fries comes with two breath mints.

If Jack Norworth were writing his classic "Take Me Out to the Ballgame" song today, he might have written "…Buy me some nachos and garlic fries, I don't care if we have cloudy skies…"

Healthy AND *Vegetarian Options*

According to the Centers for Disease Control and Prevention, just over two-thirds of adults and children in the United States today are overweight or obese. This has led to a call by many organizations for healthier eating habits and has become a major emphasis for First Lady Michelle Obama. The United States Department of Agriculture created the website *www.choosemyplate.gov* to promote healthy eating habits. A 2008 study published by *Vegetarian Times* reports that over 30 million Americans are either vegetarians or follow a vegetarian-inclined diet. Ballpark concessionaires have acknowledged this trend by increasing the variety of healthy and vegetarian options available at their food stands.

One of the pioneers in convincing the major ballpark concessionaires to offer a veggie dog alternative to the hot dog was actress Johanna McCloy (Ensign Calloway in *Star Trek: The Next Generation*). Veggie Happy (the organization started by McCloy and originally known as Soy Happy) states that its members are "advocates for vegetarian/vegan options on mainstream concession menus and…known for opening the door to vegetarian hot dogs and frankfurters at MLB [major league baseball] stadiums."

In 2005 RFK Stadium, then home of the Washington Nationals, was the first major league venue to offer a veggie dog. Rob Sunday, Aramark Resident District Manager, noted "Aramark is pleased to announce vegetarian hot dogs to our baseball fans at RFK. Aramark understands that the palate of today's fan is more diverse than ever and takes great pride in offering options that reflect these expanding tastes. Through consulting with the advocacy service, Soy Happy, Aramark believes that offering veggie dogs at RFK is an idea whose time has come."

From this beginning, there has been an expansion of healthy and vegetarian foods introduced at ballparks around the country. The following are a sampling of what one can find at major league ballparks today.

Grilled Vegetable Panini at Angel Stadium (Los Angeles Angels of Anaheim) is made with zucchini, carrots, mushrooms, tomatoes, and pesto sauce

Vegetarian Sushi at Great American Ballpark (Cincinnati Reds)

South Beach Fruit Salad at Marlins Park (Miami Marlins) contains fresh local fruits including grapefruit, watermelon, pineapple, mango, and yellow pear tomato

Portobello Sandwich at Fenway Park (Boston Red Sox) has a large portobello mushroom topped with arugula, tomato jam, and fried onions

Roasted Tomato Hummus with Pita Chips (a Mediterranean dish) at Petco Park (San Diego Padres)

Wild Pacific Salmon at PNC Park (Pittsburgh Pirates), roasted on a cedar plank and seasoned with sea salt and cracked black pepper

Roasted Vegetable Spinach Wrap at Globe Life Park in Arlington (Texas Rangers)

Veggie Kabobs at Target Field (Minnesota Twins) include summer squash and bell peppers, seasoned with pesto

Mushroom Quesadilla at Turner Field (Atlanta Braves)

Edamame at AT&T Park (San Francisco Giants)

South Beach Fruit Salad at Marlins Park, Miami, FL.

Portobello Mushroom Sandwich at Fenway Park, Boston, MA.

Kosher Food AND Knishes

The Jewish Virtual Library estimated the American Jewish population in 2012 to be 6.7 million. Sources estimate around 20% of that population observes kosher dietary laws. The majority of Jews who keep kosher live in the Northeast, Southern Florida, major Midwestern cities, or the Los Angeles area.

To be certified kosher, all ingredients in every product, and the process of preparing the product, must be certified for kosher compliance. Several major league ballparks now offer kosher food.

Kosher hot dogs, Italian sausages, pretzels, peanuts, and beer can be found at Oriole Park at Camden Yards. The Miami Marlins park features a concession stand called "Kosher Korner" with hamburgers, cheeseburgers (with soy cheese), corned beef sandwiches and potato knishes. Kosher stands can also be found at Citi Field and Yankee Stadium in New York, Dodger Stadium in Los Angeles, and other venues.

At Fenway Park in Boston, fans have access to a kosher vending machine dispensing hot dogs and knishes. The vending machine is provided by Hot Nosh Boston, a company founded by Wayne Feder, an avid sports fan and orthodox Jew. Feder often had trouble finding kosher food at sporting events, so he decided to invest in a machine that provides quick access to hot, fresh kosher food.

Hot Nosh Boston, as well as other companies including Kosher Sports Inc. and Keep It Kosher LLC, subcontract with the major concession companies to provide their kosher products.

I grew up in California and visited my Aunt Sylvie and Uncle Abe in New York City almost every summer. One of my fondest memories is eating knishes sold at that time from street corner carts. I also enjoyed knishes when Uncle Abe took me to see the New York Mets play at Shea Stadium.

A knish is a Jewish snack food made popular in North America by Eastern European immigrants. It consists of a filling covered with dough that is baked, grilled, or deep fried. Although knishes can have a variety of fillings, the most common is potato. I believe a knish is a perfect baseball snack food. It is a non-messy finger food that allows for concentrating on the game while eating. When prepared like my mother used to make, the potato filling would literally melt in your mouth.

Kosher food is tasty and healthy. Lenny Kohn (of Kohn's Kosher Deli) runs a kosher stand at Busch Stadium in St. Louis and estimates that 95% of his customers are non-kosher. They simply prefer the kosher food for its taste and quality.

Health Magazine produced a feature on its website entitled "Healthy Eats at 30 Major League Baseball Parks." At only 180 calories the magazine's healthy choice for Citi Field in New York was the potato knish.

**Potato Knish at Yankee Stadium,
New York, NY.**

OFFICIAL

Cheese Doodle

OF THE NEW YORK METS

On June 15, 2005, Cheez Doodles, manufactured by Wise Foods Inc., became the official cheese doodle of the New York Mets. "Our partnership with Wise snacks is a home run," said Mets Senior Executive Vice President Jeff Wilpon. "Nothing signals the arrival of summer more than watching Mets baseball and enjoying delicious Wise snacks." To this day, Cheez Doodles remains the official cheese doodle of the New York Mets.

For those of you not familiar with cheese doodles, they are a snack food made with corn meal that has been puffed, baked, and coated with cheddar cheese. Morrie Yohai invented the cheese doodle in the 1940s. After serving in the U.S. Marines in World War II, he returned home to the Bronx, New York, and took over his family's snack food business. The business was later purchased by Wise Foods. Today over 15 million pounds of Cheez Doodles are manufactured each year.

According to Hallmark, March 5 is National Cheese Doodle Day. This corresponds to the approximate start of spring exhibition games. It is hard to determine which of these events is more highly anticipated by baseball fans.

Bag of Cheez Doodles. Courtesy of Wise Foods Inc.

Now that you know more about cheese doodles than you ever wanted to know, are you wondering what the function of an "official" cheese doodle is versus an "unofficial" cheese doodle? Do you want to understand how other major league teams cope without an official cheese doodle? As with the mystery surrounding the invention of the hot dog, we may never know the answer.

THE BIG SIX AND THE BUSINESS OF

In certain American consumer markets, a limited number of companies dominate a large share of that particular market. The majority of cellular phone service is provided by Verizon, AT&T, Sprint, or T-Mobile. Most of the breakfast cereals sold in grocery stores are products manufactured by Kellogg, General Mills, Post, or Quaker. A similar situation exists with major league baseball concessionaires.

Concessions services at all 30 major league parks are provided by six companies: Aramark, Delaware North Companies, Levy Restaurants, Centerplate, Legends, and Ovations Food Services.

Aramark

Atlanta Braves (Turner Field)

Boston Red Sox (Fenway Park)

Colorado Rockies (Coors Field)

Houston Astros (Minute Maid Park)

Kansas City Royals (Kauffman Stadium)

New York Mets (Citi Field)

Philadelphia Phillies (Citizens Bank Park)

Pittsburgh Pirates (PNC Park) -- [except luxury suites and club restaurants]

Toronto Blue Jays (Rogers Centre)

Delaware North Companies

Baltimore Orioles (Oriole Park at Camden Yards)

Cincinnati Reds (Great American Ball Park)

Cleveland Indians (Progressive Field)

Delaware North Companies continued

Detroit Tigers (Comerica Park)

Milwaukee Brewers (Miller Park)

Minnesota Twins (Target Field)

San Diego Padres (Petco Park)

St. Louis Cardinals (Busch Stadium)

Texas Rangers (Globe Life Park in Arlington)

Levy Restaurants

Arizona Diamondbacks (Chase Field)

Chicago Cubs (Wrigley Field)

Chicago White Sox (U.S. Cellular Field)

Los Angeles Dodgers (Dodger Stadium)

Miami Marlins (Marlins Park)

Pittsburgh Pirates (PNC Park) -- [luxury suites and club restaurants only]

Washington Nationals (Nationals Park)

Centerplate

San Francisco Giants (AT&T Park)

Seattle Mariners (Safeco Field)

Tampa Bay Rays (Tropicana Field)

Legends

Los Angeles Angels of Anaheim (Angel Stadium of Anaheim)

New York Yankees (Yankee Stadium)

Ovations Food Services

Oakland Athletics (O.co Coliseum)

Additionally, these six companies have the concessions contracts for many minor league baseball teams as well as at other sport venues. Some minor league teams handle their concessions in-house, without contracting with an outside company.

Aramark Corporation provides food service and facilities management to businesses, educational institutions, prisons, and health care institutions, as well as sports facilities. It is headquartered in Philadelphia, Pennsylvania, and had annual 2012 revenues of 13.5 billion dollars. Aramark was founded in 1936 by brothers Davre and Henry Davidson, who started with vending services for employees in Southern California's aviation industry. By purchasing Harry M. Stevens, Inc. in 1994, the company increased their ballpark presence.

Delaware North (also known by one of its division names, Sportservice) is a food service and hospitality company that operates hotels as well as concessions at airports, gaming and entertainment venues, and sports venues. It is headquartered in Buffalo, New York, and had annual 2012 revenues of 2.6 billion dollars. Delaware North was founded in 1915 by brothers Charles, Marvin, and Louis Jacobs, who started selling peanuts at Coney Island in New York, and then expanded to the Buffalo Bisons' ballpark.

Levy Restaurants specializes in providing vending and food services to entertainment and sports venues. It is based in Chicago, Illinois, and is a subsidiary of Compass Group, a British multinational contract food service and support services company. Levy Restaurants was founded by Larry Levy who began with D.B. Kaplan's Delicatessen in Chicago in 1978. In 1982 his company obtained the concessions contract at Comiskey Park, then home of the Chicago White Sox. In 1985 it got the contract for the Chicago Cubs at Wrigley Field. In 2006 Levy Restaurants was purchased by Compass Group.

In 2012 annual revenues for Compass Group were 27.4 billion dollars.

Although **Centerplate** serves only three major league baseball parks, it is the largest food service provider to the teams of the National Football League as well as to soccer teams in the United Kingdom. Centerplate was formerly known as Volume Services America and was a division of the Flagstar Companies. In 1995 Flagstar sold Volume Services to the Blackstone Group. The name was changed to Centerplate in 2004. In 2009 it became an independent privately-owned company headquartered in Spartanburg, South Carolina. The company traces its roots back to 1929 when Nathaniel Leverone founded the Automated Canteen Company of America, selling candy bars, nuts and chewing gum from vending machines.

Legends, the smallest of the six major league ballpark concessionaires, is jointly owned by the New York Yankees, the Dallas Cowboys football team, and Checketts Partners Investment Fund. The company acquired the contract for a second major league baseball park when the Los Angeles Angels signed with Legends to replace Aramark at the end of the 2013 season. Headquartered in New York City, Legends has been selected to operate the observation deck opening in 2015 at the top of One World Trade Center.

Ovations Food Services provides food and beverage service to arenas, stadiums, amphitheaters, fairgrounds, and convention centers throughout the country. Although it has served AAA teams including the Fresno Grizzlies at Chukchansi Park and the Sacramento River Cats at Raley Field, its January 2014 contract with the Oakland A's is its first with a major league team. Ovations Food Services is a subsidiary of Comcast Spectacor, a global leader in the sports management industry. Comcast Spectacor in turn is a subsidiary of Comcast Corporation, the nation's largest video and high-speed Internet provider.

A recent trend in ballpark food service is to have well-known local restaurants or brands represented in the concession options. Ghirardelli Chocolate Company provides sundaes at AT&T Park in San Francisco. Seattle's Ivar's Seafood Restaurant offers its famous clam chowder at Safeco Field. Nathan's Famous hot dogs are sold at Yankee Stadium. In most cases the local restaurant or brand contracts directly with the ballpark's concessionaire.

According to *SportsBusiness Journal*, annual revenue from on-site game day concessions in 2012 was 10.7 billion dollars. This included football, basketball, and hockey as well as baseball venues. Aramark revenues accounted for 31% of the market, Levy Restaurants had 24%, Delaware North had 19%, and Centerplate had 16%. (Figures are not available for Legends and Ovations Food Services.)

During the era of traditional ballpark food (approximately 1900 to 1980), Harry M. Stevens was a giant in the business. However, his lifetime revenues represent only a small fraction of the big business of ballpark concessions today.

Colorful Vendors

Fans at baseball games are accustomed to seeing food vendors making their way throughout the stands, climbing up and down the steep stairs as they call out their wares and pass the purchased products down the row of seats. Some vendors are particularly good at attracting attention by their dress or actions.

The tradition of colorful vendors hawking their goods goes back all the way to Harry M. Stevens himself. In his red coat and straw hat, Stevens was a noticeable figure in the ballpark stands, quoting Shakespeare and Byron as he offered his scorecards and food for sale.

The best-known vendor of modern times is Roger Owens of Dodger Stadium, known as "The Peanut Man." Roger has worked at Dodger Stadium from its opening in 1962 until the present day. He became known for his trick tossing of peanut bags to customers up to 30 rows away. His antics gained him much renown including an appearance on *The Tonight Show Starring Johnny Carson* in 1976. Although many ballplayers have had biographies written about them, Roger Owens may be the only peanut vendor to have achieved this honor. *The Perfect Pitch: The Biography of Roger Owens, The Famous Peanut Man at Dodger Stadium,* by Daniel S. Green, was published in 2004.

At the age of 24 in 1938, Dan Ferrone was picked from among hundreds of young men waiting for a vending job with the Chicago Cubs at Wrigley Field. Although he had other jobs as well, he remained at Wrigley Field until 1995. He was a familiar face to generations of fans as he peddled first programs, then beer and peanuts. Sadly, during his 58-year career, he never was able to watch the Cubs win a World Series.

Hot dog vendor Charley Marcuse worked for the Detroit Tigers for the last decade. He was known as the "Singing Hot Dog Man" for singing the words "hot dog" in operatic falsetto. He was also known for his adamant dislike of ketchup, wanting all of his customers to put mustard on their hot dogs. This condiment controversy led to a dispute with management and to Charley leaving the Tigers in 2013.

Fans in the outfield bleachers at Coors Field in Denver are served by beer vendor Brent Doeden, also known as "Captain Earthman." He hands out cards with both his cell phone number and his planetary location number. No one quite knows what it means, but he has many loyal customers.

In the 1970s at the Texas Rangers Arlington Stadium, Ray Jones was known as "The Birdman of Pennants." Jones used a bird call to attract attention to the banners he was selling. He also made a yelping sound like a dog and performed "The Eyes of Texas" in a shrill whistle.

Many other vendors find subtle ways to attract customers. At a recent Arizona Diamondbacks game we attended, the man with a tray of drink cups bellowed out "Lemonade, lemonade, just like your grandma made." Both my wife and I bought his lemonade.

"The Peanut Man," Roger Owens. Courtesy of Roger Owens.

OF THE MAJOR LEAGUE BALLPARKS

To paraphrase Laozi and Mao Zedong, a journey of 30 ballparks begins with a single hot dog. During the 2014 baseball season my wife and I traveled to each of the major league stadiums to investigate the variety of food offerings from hot dogs and sausages to the specialities of the new food era.

In the early days, when baseball was becoming the American national pastime, a fan who wanted a hot dog at the ballpark got just that -- a hot dog. There was no choice; a hot dog was a hot dog. Times have changed. *The Great American Hot Dog Book: Recipes and Side Dishes From Across America*, by Becky Mercuri, includes hot dog recipes from every state in the union. Many ballparks have signature hot dogs as well as a variety of other hot dogs from which to choose.

Still not convinced that you want a hot dog? You have many other choices. Some stadiums have gone all out to showcase unique, gourmet-style food. Many parks emphasize regional food as well as having offerings from well-known local restaurants. There are also several ballparks where retired ballplayers are shaping new careers as signature food purveyors.

Some stadiums have luxury levels open only to fans who have purchased the most expensive seats. I have elected not to include concession stands located on these luxury levels. I have also chosen not to include sit-down restaurants located inside a ballpark. Instead the focus is on food available to general ticketed fans throughout the ballpark.

My culinary tour is not intended to be comprehensive nor a ratings guide, but rather to celebrate the variety of foods now available at major league ballparks. The era of hot dogs, peanuts and Cracker Jack alone is now just a memory, as you will soon discover.

ARIZONA DIAMONDBACKS

Chase Field opened in 1998 and has been the only home of the Diamondbacks since they were added to the National League as an expansion team. The field was one of the first major league stadiums built with a retractable roof.

Featured Hot Dog/Sausage

The Venom Dog is named after the venomous nature of the western diamondback rattlesnake. The Venom Dog is a specially-crafted habanero sausage with black beans, pico de gallo, and sour cream. Habanero is a very hot chili pepper that originated many centuries ago in the Amazon region of South America.

Venom Dog

More Hot Dogs and Sausages

The Sonoran Dog gives fans a taste of old Mexico. Mesquite-smoked bacon is grilled and wrapped around a hot dog, which is then topped with pico de gallo and ranch-style beans. Mayonnaise is drizzled over the top. This special hot dog gets its name from the Mexican state of Sonora where it originated.

The D-Bat corn dog, at 18 inches long, is the Diamondbacks contribution to the supersize trend. The hot dog is filled with cheddar cheese, bacon, and jalapeños, coated in cornmeal batter and deep fried, then served on a bed of French fries.

Macayo's Mexican Kitchen

The first Macayo's restaurant opened in 1946 in the Phoenix area. Still owned and operated by the Macayo family, there are now 14 Macayo locations in Arizona, including one at Chase Field. A wide variety of burritos, tacos and fajitas are offered. The Macayo Bowl contains your choice of chicken or beef, rice, beans, cheese, sour cream, guacamole, and pico de gallo. Here you can also get spinach con queso (spinach cheese dip).

Fatburger

Although founded in Los Angeles, the first Fatburger at a ballpark opened in 2008 at Chase Field. The iconic hamburger chain was started in 1946 by Lovie Yancey. Today Fatburgers can be found

Fatburger D-backs Double Cheeseburger

in over 30 countries around the world. Magic Johnson, Queen Latifah, Kanye West, and Montel Williams have all, at one point, been involved in the ownership or operation of Fatburger franchises. The D-backs Double cheeseburger features two one-third pound patties and two slices of cheese with lettuce, tomatoes, and onions on a toasted bun. In addition to the beef burgers Fatburger also offers a turkey burger.

Rey Gloria

Rey Gloria's Tamale Stand is run by former Diamondback security guard Rey Cota. In 2006 Diamondback president Derrick Hall tasted one of Rey's tamales, and he liked it so much that he offered his employee a stand at Chase Field. Cota's red chili and green corn tamales are based on a recipe from his mother, Gloria.

Bisbee Tamale

Vegans can find a tamale to their liking known as the Bisbee Tamale provided by the Tucson Tamale Company. It is stuffed with soy chorizo, potatoes, and pinto beans, and served with guacamole and salsa roja (made from red chilies and tomatillos).

Bisbee Tamale

Antipasto and Greek Salads

At the Streets of New York pizza stand, two specialty salads are offered. The antipasto salad has capicola ham, Genoa salami, pepperoni, tomatoes, cucumbers, bell peppers, black and green olives, pepperocini (a mild yellowish-green pepper), and includes a homemade Italian dressing. The Greek salad contains romaine lettuce, tomatoes, cucumbers, bell peppers, red onions, Kalamata olives, feta cheese, and comes with a traditional Greek dressing.

Caramel Apples and New York Cheesecake

Whoever first said "An apple a day keeps the doctor away" probably wasn't thinking about caramel apples. These colorful treats on sticks can be ordered with caramel alone, with additional nuts, or with either chocolate or rainbow sprinkles.

For many people, New York brings up images of the Statue of Liberty or the Empire State Building. But for cheesecake lovers the first thing that comes to mind is New York-style cheesecake. New York cheesecake is rich with a dense, smooth, and creamy consistency. The Streets of New York stand at Chase Field serves its slices with cherry sauce.

New York Cheesecake

ATLANTA BRAVES

Turner Field was originally built as Centennial Olympic Stadium in 1996 as part of the Summer Olympic Games in Atlanta. The field is named for Ted Turner, founder of CNN cable news network and former owner of the Atlanta Braves. The Braves are planning to build a new stadium in suburban Cobb County. Completion is expected in 2016.

Featured Hot Dog/Sausage

The Taste of the Majors stand at Turner Field features two Southern-themed hot dogs. One is the Dixie Dog which is twelve inches long, weighs one-half pound, and (reflecting its Southern heritage) is flash fried. Then it's topped with pulled pork, cole slaw, pickles and barbeque sauce.

Dixie Dog

More Hot Dogs and Sausages

The Taste of the Majors also offers the Georgia Dog with cole slaw, relish, and Vidalia onions. Vidalia onions, the official state vegetable of Georgia since 1990, were developed accidentally in Georgia during the Great Depression. When farmers planted onions in Georgia's sandy soil, what grew was a strange onion that was sweeter than ordinary onions. The sweet onion was promoted by the Piggly Wiggly grocery store chain, which was headquartered in the town of Vidalia.

One of the hot dog stands at Turner Field is called Nat's Grand Slam Franks Trolley Car 207, and is shaped like a trolley car. The Nat's is for National Deli, the provider of Turner Field hot dogs. After extensive research, I could find no significance to the number 207, but the red trolley car design is eye-catching.

Waffle House

Waffle House restaurants, founded in 1955, are located throughout the South. On the *www.oneforthetable.com* website, Ann Nichols refers to the Waffle House as the "unofficial flower of the Southern interstate exit." Since 1955 the over 1,500 Waffle House restaurants have served 880 million waffles and 1.3 billion cups of coffee. The Waffle House at Turner Field serves its classic waffle, chocolate chip waffle, and peanut butter waffle. The popular Double Hash Browns come with onions, cheese, ham, and peppers.

Chocolate Chip Waffle

Holeman & Finch Public House

Atlanta's Holeman & Finch Public House (called H&F) is known for its handcrafted double patty cheeseburgers served each night at 10 PM. Only 24 burgers are prepared each night, and are reserved ahead of time by discerning customers. Now burger fans have another opportunity to purchase these burgers at the H&F Stand at Turner Field, where larger numbers of the famous cheeseburger are served up, along with homemade French fries.

Kevin Rathbun

Restaurateur and chef Kevin Rathbun owns three award-winning restaurants in Atlanta. His restaurants have been featured in *The New York Times* and *USA Today* as well as on the *The Today Show* and *Good Morning America*. Mr. Rathbun has worked with well-known chefs including Emeril Lagasse. Kevin Rathbun Steak at Turner Field serves two items: a steak sandwich and a Big Kev. The Big Kev is a double steak sandwich for those who want a pound of meat. A viewing window beside the Kevin Rathbun Steak stand allows customers to watch a butcher cutting the steaks.

Mayfield Dairy Farms

In 1910, T. B. Mayfield, Jr., purchased 45 Jersey cows and began delivering milk to customers in his hometown of Athens, Tennessee (about 150 miles north of Atlanta.) Today Scottie and Rob Mayfield are the fourth generation of the Mayfield family to run Mayfield Dairy Farms. Its well-known ice cream is served at Turner Field in 13 flavors including chocolate chip cookie dough, and butter pecan.

Frozen Pints

Frozen Pints produces craft beer ice cream. According to their creators, "Someone spilled a beer near the ice cream maker, and in a moment of slightly inebriated inspiration, we found our calling." Four flavors are offered at the Turner Field stand: peach lambic (light, tart, sweet peach, champagne-like); vanilla bock (creamy vanilla, hints of banana and clove); brown ale chip (hints of roasted hazelnut, dark chocolate chip); malted milk chocolate stout (chocolate malted milk, hints of coffee.) The alcohol by volume (ABV) is between 1% and 2% and fans must be at least 21 years of age in order to purchase the ice cream.

Yicketty Yamwich

Chipper Jones and the Yicketty Yamwich

The term "yicketty" means to hit a home run. It was first introduced by Atlanta Braves third baseman Chipper Jones via a July 25, 2012, tweet. Chipper, who retired in 2012, played his entire 20-year career with the Atlanta Braves and holds the team record for career on-base percentage. In honor of Chipper Jones is the Yicketty Yamwich. The Yamwich contains boneless short ribs, Brie cheese, apple butter spread, baby spinach, and cheddar cheese, a combination not likely found elsewhere in a sandwich.

Cinnamon-Glazed Pecans

According to the United States Department of Agriculture, Georgia is the leading producer of pecans with over 40% of the nation's crop. Turner Field offers fresh, warm cinnamon-glazed pecans. Fans can watch the pecans swirling in the mixer while they are being glazed.

Cinnamon-Glazed Pecans

BALTIMORE ORIOLES

Oriole Park at Camden Yards opened in 1992. It was built at the beginning of the "retro" major league ballpark trend that occurred during the 1990s and early 2000s in which the ballparks were built for baseball only and each park has a unique character. It is believed that Babe Ruth's father once owned a saloon on a plot of land that is now center field of Oriole Park.

Birdland Hot Dog

Featured Hot Dog/Sausage

Baltimore Magazine refers to Stuggy's as a "Baltimore institution." Stuggy's restaurants are located in the Fell's Point and Federal Hill neighborhoods of Baltimore. In a mission to create the most delicious and nutritious hot dog for their hometown of Baltimore, a father and son traveled to many countries researching hot dogs. They came up with an all-beef, gluten-free, kosher-style hot dog that has become an area favorite. At the Stuggy's stand at Oriole Park, fans can try some unique creations. The Birdland Hot Dog has smoked brisket, pepperoni hash, tomato jam, and frizzled onions on top of the hot dog.

More Hot Dogs and Sausages

Two other hot dogs of note are available at the Stuggy's stand. The Crab Mac 'N Cheese Hot Dog, as its name suggests, is covered with crab and macaroni and cheese. The Early Bird Hot Dog comes with a fried egg, cheddar cheese and crispy bacon.

The Sausage Haus serves Natty Boh bratwurst. Natty Boh is short for National Bohemian (a local beer that was first brewed in Baltimore in 1885) which is added to the German-style handmade bratwurst.

Polock Johnny's has been serving Polish sausages in Baltimore since the early part of the twentieth century. Since 1921 its motto has been "Polock Johnny is my name; Polish sausage is my game." "Polock" is an alternate spelling of "polack" which the *American Heritage Dictionary* refers to as "offensive." Polock Johnny's Polish sausage comes with "the works": green peppers, onions, cucumbers, celery, and relish.

The traditional hot dogs at Oriole Park are made by Esskay. Esskay was founded in 1858 by German immigrant William Schluderberg. Esskay has been a leader in marketing innovation, being the first company to feature the Muppets puppets in its advertisements. Esskay remained an independent company for 127 years, until it was sold in 1985 to Smithfield Foods.

Gino's Hamburgers

Gino's Hamburgers was a fast food restaurant chain founded in Baltimore by Baltimore Colts' defensive end Gino Marchetti and running back Alan Ameche. The chain had grown to 359 restaurants when it was purchased by the Marriott Corporation in 1982. Marriott discontinued the brand and converted the locations to Roy Rogers Restaurants. A new version known as Gino's Burgers and Chicken was opened in 2010 by Tom Romano, who was chief operating officer of Gino's Hamburgers in 1982 when the chain was sold. At Oriole Park, Gino's serves hamburgers and chicken tenders. The Camden Giant Burger has a crab cake on top of the hamburger. The Bang Bang Chipotle Burger comes with fried onions and jalapeños.

Soft-Shell Crab Sandwich and Maryland Crab Soup

Soft-Shell Crab Sandwich

The Old Bay Seafood stand features products made with Old Bay seasoning. For over 70 years, the Old Bay seasoning's blend of 18 spices and herbs has brought the flavor of the Chesapeake Bay area to the rest of the country. At Oriole Park, along with traditional crab cakes, fans can sample a soft-shell crab sandwich and Maryland crab soup. For marine biologists, a soft-shell crab is a crab which has recently molted its exoskeleton; for the rest of us, this means almost the entire crab can be eaten rather than having to shell the crab first in order to reach the meat. The soft-shell crab sandwich is served with a choice of cocktail or tartar sauce.

Maryland crab soup is made from blue crabs found along the mouth of Chesapeake Bay in Virginia and North Carolina. It was first made by Native Americans who lived along these shores. They would combine the crab meat with vegetables and steam them together in large pots.

Flying Dog

In 1983 George Stranahan climbed the dangerous K2 peak in Pakistan, the second highest mountain in the world. Later while out having a drink and celebrating his success, he happened to notice a large oil painting of a dog that appeared to be flying. At this point, you are probably asking what this has to do with ballpark food in Baltimore. The answer is: in 1990 Stranahan founded a brewpub in Aspen, Colorado, and named it the Flying Dog. Later he opened a full-fledged brewery in Denver. (We're still not to the Baltimore ballpark, but we're getting there.) In 1994 the brewery moved to Frederick, Maryland. Finally, back at Oriole Park, the Flying Dog Brewery stand offers Chesapeake Waffle Fries. Its fries are topped with a crab dip made with Old Bay seasoning.

Boog Powell's BBQ

Boog Powell was a first baseman with the Baltimore Orioles from 1961-74. He won the American League Most Valuable Player Award in 1970. He later appeared in television commercials for Miller Lite Beer. Boog is now the owner of Boog's BBQ serving beef, pork and turkey sandwiches. The beef sandwich is Maryland pit beef (charcoal-grilled top roast, sliced thinly), a regional specialty.

Boog's Pit Beef Sandwich

Jack Daniels

The Jack Daniels stand, in addition to selling whiskey drinks, offers pulled pork sandwiches, hot dogs, and bacon on a stick. For fans who can't make up their minds, the Triple Crown Sandwich is available featuring pulled pork, a grilled hot dog and bacon on a stick combined into a pork lover's delight.

Tako Korean BBQ

According to the 2010 Census, Baltimore has the third largest Korean-American population in the United States. Tako Korean BBQ at Oriole Park serves Kogi beef and Kogi chicken takos. The shell in which the tako is served is similar to that of the Mexican soft taco, reflecting the fusion of Korean and Mexican food found in the taco food trucks of the Los Angeles area. The takos come with a choice of sweet Asian slaw or kimchi. Kimchi is a traditional fermented Korean side dish usually made from cabbage. Also available are steamed Asian buns filled with either barbequed pork or edamame, and Pad Thai Cold Noodle Salad.

Kogi Chicken Takos

Reuben Sandwich

The Baseline Chop House stand serves a traditional Reuben sandwich. A Reuben sandwich contains corned beef, Swiss cheese, Russian dressing and sauerkraut, all grilled and served on rye bread. Two stories exist as to the origin of the Reuben name. One holds that Reuben Kulakofsky was the inventor as part of a group effort by members of his weekly poker game held in the Blackstone Hotel in Omaha, Nebraska, during the 1920s. Another account says that the sandwich was created in 1914 by Arnold Reuben, a New York City delicatessen owner. As is the case with the origin of the hot dog, we may never know for sure.

BOSTON RED SOX

Fenway Park, built in 1912, is the oldest stadium in the major leagues. Although its age contributes to the old-time charm, it limits the amount of space for food concessions. As a result, nearly all the food booths are on the concourse level or on Yawkey Way just outside the park. During games, Yawkey Way is considered part of the stadium and can be accessed only with a game ticket.

Featured Hot Dog/Sausage

The Fenway Frank (along with the Dodger Dog) is the best known of the "classic" ballpark hot dogs. It is made by Kayem Foods in nearby Chelsea. Kayem Foods was founded in a small storefront in 1909 by Polish immigrants Kazimierz and Helena Monkiewicz. The hot dog is boiled and grilled and served on a traditional New England-style bun (crustless on the side with a split top). Fenway Franks are sold throughout the ballpark. The Monster Dog is an extra-large version of the Fenway Frank.

Fenway Frank

More Hot Dogs and Sausages

Located on Yawkey Way is The Best Sausage Company. It's hard to miss this stand when its employee, wearing a oversized sausage hat, is actively waving and hawking at potential customers. The sausage varieties are Italian (sweet or hot), Cajun, or chicken. It also serves steak tips and pepperoni pizza. I noticed that The Best Sausage Company did not serve sausage pizza, and I inquired about this. I was told that they grill the sausage but they are not going to bother putting it on pizza. (Maybe one has to be a native New Englander to understand this).

Legal Sea Foods

The Fenway Fish Shack features sea food from Legal Sea Foods, a Cambridge, Massachusetts, restaurant and fish market run by the Berkowitz family. The "Legal" part of the name comes not from any law but from the connection of the original family grocery store with Legal Stamps (an early trading stamp incentive for cash-paying customers). At the Fenway Fish Shack fans can get fish and chips, fish sandwiches, fried clams, and clam chowder. With the slogan "If it isn't fresh, it isn't Legal," you can count on having fresh fish every time.

Nicky's Peanut Wagon

Nicky's Peanut Wagon can be found at the entry to Yawkey Way. Nicky's grandfather George began the family peanut business in 1912. In addition to fresh roasted peanuts, Nicky sells pistachios, cashews, salted almonds, and honey-roasted peanuts.

Pork Jerky

In addition to the normal packaged snack items such as Cracker Jack and candy bars, stands throughout Fenway sell Krave pork jerky. According to the Krave website, 2014 Boston Marathon winner Meb Keflezighi trained on Krave jerky products.

Whoopie Pie

Besides ice cream, Scoop Scoop Scoop sells the New England dessert favorite, Whoopie Pie, the "official state treat" of Maine. Said to have originated with the Pennsylvania Amish, the Whoopie Pie has two rounded mounds of cake (usually chocolate) with a cream filling between them.

Whoopie Pie

El Tiante

The El Tiante stand is named for former Boston Red Sox pitcher Luis Tiant, known as El Tiante. Tiant, a native of Cuba, pitched the opening game of the 1975 World Series after having a stunning year for the Red Sox. The signature item offered at the El Tiante stand is the Cuban sandwich: layers of ham, pork, cheese, pickles and mustard on a grilled bun.

World Fare

Sandwich lovers have several choices at Fenway's World Fare. Choices include corned beef on marble rye; hot Reuben with sauerkraut, Russian dressing, and Swiss cheese; hot pastrami with spicy mustard; and hot Italian beef *au jus* served with fresh mozzarella and banana peppers.

Cuban Sandwich

Lobster Roll

The Home Plate Grill serves the traditional New England lobster roll, with the lobster meat soaked in butter and placed in a steamed roll with the opening on the top. According to *The Encyclopedia of American Food and Drink* by John F. Mariani, the lobster roll was created at Perry's restaurant in Milford, Connecticut, in the 1920s.

Lobster Roll

Visitors Veggies

Located on the visitors' side of the concourse is Visitors Veggies. Veggie burgers, veggie dogs, and hummus and chips can be found there. Is it located on the visitors' side because true members of Red Sox Nation don't like their veggies?

Big Concourse Sandwiches

Big Concourse Sandwiches features two interesting specialties. The Breakfast Burger is a hamburger patty topped with a fried egg, fresh mozzarella and spicy chipotle sauce. The Portobello Sandwich has a large portobello mushroom topped with arugula, tomato jam, and fried onions.

Kosher Vending Machine

Although there is not a kosher stand at Fenway Park, there is a kosher vending machine which dispenses hot cheese pizza slices, mozzarella sticks, pizza pockets, onion rings, and potato knishes. It is the only kosher vending machine located at a major league ballpark.

Fenway Fry Bar

The Fenway Fry Bar sells French fries with a variety of interesting toppings: baked beans, poutine gravy, chili con carne, and nacho cheese. It also sell Fenway Spiral Fries which are spiral-shaped potato chips served on a wooden skewer.

CHICAGO CUBS

Wrigley Field opened in 1914 and is celebrating its centennial in 2014. The stadium is known for its ivy-covered outfield wall. Wrigley Field and Boston's Fenway Park are the only stadiums remaining from the early days of the American and National Leagues. However, unlike Fenway Park, Wrigley Field is still waiting to see its first World Series championship home team.

TV Dinner Dog

Featured Hot Dog/Sausage

The Decade Dogs stand celebrates the history of Wrigley Field by offering hot dogs from various decades. The 1950s dog is the TV Dinner Dog. The TV dinner was first introduced by Swanson in 1954. It fulfilled two post-war trends: interest in time-saving activities and fascination with television. Swanson's sold over ten million TV dinners in its first year. The TV Dinner Dog is topped with mashed potatoes, corn, fried onions, and gravy.

More Hot Dogs and Sausages

Other Decade Dogs include the 1910s Reuben Dog topped with sliced corned beef, sauerkraut, Thousand Island dressing, and Swiss cheese. The 1920s Chicago Dog comes with tomato wedges, pickle spears, diced onions, neon-green relish, sport peppers, mustard and celery salt on a poppy seed bun. The 1960s Buffalo Wing Dog is topped with diced chicken, buffalo sauce, and blue cheese slaw. Finally, the 1970s Pulled Pork Dog is covered with pulled pork, cole slaw, and barbeque sauce.

Vienna Beef provides the beef hot dogs and sausages at Wrigley Field. Vienna Beef hot dogs were first introduced at the 1893 Chicago Columbian Exposition by Austrian immigrants Emil Reichel and Sam Ladany. They opened their first store in 1894 on Chicago's Near West Side and began selling their products to other restaurants and markets in 1900. It remains, 121 years later, Chicago's best-selling and best known hot dogs.

The Maxwell Street Polish consists of a fried Polish sausage topped with grilled onions, green peppers, and yellow mustard. It traces its origins back to Chicago's Maxwell Street Market, where the sandwich was created by Jimmy Stefanovic at his hot dog stand in 1939. *Chicago Sun-Times* food writer Sandy Thorne Clark called the Maxwell Street Polish "a classic food synonymous with Chicago." Fans at Wrigley Field can order this classic at the Big Dawgs stand.

Chicagoans and visitors are not limited to Vienna Beef hot dogs and sausages. High Plains Bison is "the official lean meat of the Chicago Cubs." Its stand at Wrigley Field offers bison hot dogs, bison bratwurst, and bison Italian sausage. Bison is naturally lean and lower in saturated fat than beef, chicken, pork, or salmon. High Plains bison graze on grasses, sagebrush, and other native vegetation, and the meat contains no additives or fillers.

Giordano's Stuffed Pizza

Chicago is known for its deep-dish pizza and its stuffed pizza. Deep-dish pizza has a very high crust creating a pizza that resembles a pie more than flatbread. Unlike other pizza, the extra ingredients (e.g. sausage or pepperoni) are layered on the crust with the sauce and cheese on top. A stuffed pizza is similar to a deep-dish pizza but with an additional layer of dough on top, covered with more tomato sauce. Giordano's may have been the originator of stuffed pizza, though there is a competing claim from Nancy's Pizza of Chicago. At Wrigley Field, Giordano's sells stuffed sausage and cheese pizzas. Giordano's has been named Chicago's best pizza by NBC, *The New York Times*, *Chicago Tribune,* and *Home & Garden Magazine*.

Uncle Dougie's Barbeque Sauce

In 1989 Chicago resident Doug Tomek invented a marinade for preparing tasty chicken wings without frying. Friends and family members loved the marinade and asked Doug to make his wings at all of their events. This encouraged Doug to start a business, and Uncle Dougie's was born. Today Uncle Dougie's produces many different marinades and sauces. Pulled pork sandwiches with Uncle Dougie's barbeque sauce are available throughout Wrigley Field.

Prairie City Bakery

Many ballparks have an official hot dog, but Wrigley Field also has an official cookie. Prairie City Bakery's Giant Chocolate Chip Cookie is indeed "the official cookie of the Chicago Cubs." Prairie City Bakery was founded in nearby Vernon Hills in 1994 by Bill Skeenes and Bob Rosean. Both Bill and Bob previously worked for Sara Lee Bakery. Today Prairie City Bakery products are found in over 20,000 locations nationwide. In addition to the chocolate chip cookie, fans at Wrigley Field can also buy a Big n' Fudgy Brownie.

Big n' Fudgy Brownie

Asian Pork Burger

A specialty item available at the Decades Diner is the Asian Pork Burger, a meat patty made with ground pork instead of beef or turkey. The burger is topped with Asian slaw (cole slaw with a sweet vinaigrette dressing) and served on a toasted Hawaiian bun. Hawaiian buns or bread have a fluffy texture and a sweet flavor. The bread is similar to Portuguese sweet bread and is believed to have been brought to Hawaii by Portuguese immigrants.

Asian Pork Burger

"Nuts On Clark"

The "Nuts On Clark" corporate offices and main retail store are located two blocks north of Wrigley Field on Clark Street. Naturally, it has a cart at Wrigley Field. But if you guessed that it sells nuts, you would be wrong. Instead it sells gourmet popcorn. Fans can get original popcorn, kettle corn, cheese corn, caramel corn, or the Chicago mix (a combination of cheese and caramel corn).

Sloppy Jane

Sloppy Jane

A Sloppy Joe is a sandwich consisting of ground beef, onions, tomato sauce, Worcestershire sauce and other seasonings served on a hamburger bun. According to *The American Century Cookbook: The Most Popular Recipes of the 20th Century* by Jean Anderson, research suggests that the Sloppy Joe began in a Sioux City, Iowa, café as a loose-meat sandwich created in 1930 by a cook named Joe. The Decades Diner offers a vegetarian version of the Sloppy Joe called a Sloppy Jane. Instead of beef, the Sloppy Jane uses tempeh, a soy product originally from Indonesia. It is made by a natural culturing and fermentation process that binds soy beans into a cake form.

Italian Beef Sandwich

The Italian Beef Sandwich is believed to have originated in Chicago in the 1930s. The beef is sliced thin and wet-roasted in beef broth with garlic, oregano, and other spices. The meat is served dripping wet and is therefore placed on a chewy bread, as a soft bread would disintegrate. The cooking process was historically a way to make less expensive and tougher cuts of beef more tender and tasty. The Hey Hey Hits Grill offers fans its version of the Italian Beef Sandwich.

Pretzel Baguettes

The Blue W stand serves two sandwiches on pretzel baguettes. Using pretzel dough in place of bread has become trendy in the fast food arena. According to the *QSR* (Quick Service Restaurants) *Magazine* website, "Quick-service restaurants across the country are capitalizing on a new pretzel-bread trend, taking one of the most popular summer snacks and working it into innovative new menu options." The Blue W offers a turkey pretzel baguette and a veggie pretzel baguette with cucumbers, lettuce, tomato and hummus.

CHICAGO WHITE SOX

U. S. Cellular Field opened in 1991 on Chicago's South Side. It holds the distinction of having the highest top row stadium seating in the major league ballparks. The park is built next to the site of the old Comiskey Park which served the White Sox from 1910 through 1990.

Featured Hot Dog/Sausage

As is the case for the Chicago Cubs at Wrigley Field, Vienna Beef provides the hot dogs at U.S. Cellular Field. The Comiskey Dog stand (named for Charles Comiskey, owner of the Chicago White Sox from 1901 to 1931) sells a traditional Chicago-style hot dog. The Vienna Beef frank is topped with mild yellow mustard, neon relish, chopped onions, tomato wedges, dill pickle spears, sport peppers, and celery salt, and served on a poppy seed bun. Neon relish is brightly colored and sweeter than ordinary pickle relish. Although the origins of neon relish are somewhat unclear, Superdawg Drive-In of Norwood Park, Illinois, claims to have been serving it since 1949 and is believed to be the first to introduce it to the Chicago-style hot dog.

Chicago-Style Hot Dog

More Hot Dogs and Sausages

Sausages, as well as pork hot dogs, are provided by The Bobak Sausage Company of Chicago. Bobak's refers to its company as "Chicago's sausageologists." (I just checked my Scrabble app but unfortunately "sausageologist" is not acceptable.) Frank Bobak immigrated to Chicago in the 1960s from Zakopane, Poland, where he was a shepherd. He began making sausages in his basement and smoked them in his garage. This arrangement worked well until one day the Chicago Fire Department came to put out a fire. This led Bobak to open a commercial location. At U.S. Cellular Field, Bobak's provides Polish sausage, Italian sausage, spicy jalapeño cheddar sausage, adobo mango chicken sausage, and bratwurst.

Beggars Pizza

Beggars Pizza has served the Chicago area since 1976. Today there are more than twenty locations throughout the area. At U.S. Cellular field fans can get either cheese, sausage, or pepperoni slices -- a much smaller selection than at its restaurants. But after all, beggars can't be choosers.

Hot Asian Buns

A bao is a ball-shaped steamed bun usually containing meat or vegetables. It originated in China as a way to help feed large groups of people. Wow Bao, with six locations in the Chicago area, advertises that it serves "hot Asian buns." The stand at U.S. Cellular Field offers chicken, barbeque pork, and veggie buns.

Hooters

Across from the "hot Asian buns" sign is the Hooters stand. (Feel free to let your mind wander.) Hooters restaurants are known for its scantily-clad female waitresses. Many individuals and organizations believe this practice is sexist and demeaning. According to the Hooters website, "Hooters girls are the very essence of Hooters. Trained to excel in customer service, they provide the energy, charisma, and engaging conversation that keep guests coming back. Much more than just a pretty face, Hooters girls have game." Although Hooters was founded in Florida, U.S. Cellular Field is the only major league stadium that offers its food. Fans have their choice of chicken wings or tenders with either barbeque, honey, or Thai sauces.

Minnie Minoso, The Cuban Comet

Minnie Minoso, born in Havana, Cuba, had a long major league career including many years with the Chicago White Sox. He is one of only two players in major league history to play in five different decades (1940s-1980s). Thirteen years after retiring in 1964, Minoso made a three-day comeback at the age of 50 with the Chicago White Sox. Four years later he made a second comeback, this one for two games, at the age of 54. Due to his great speed, he was nicknamed "The Cuban Comet." The Cuban Comet stand at U.S. Cellular Field sells a pressed hot Cuban sandwich made from sliced ham, shredded pork, Swiss cheese, mustard, sliced pickles and mojo sauce. Mojo sauce consists of olive oil, salt, water, garlic, paprika, coriander, and local pepper varieties.

Pork Chop Sandwich

The South Side Hitmen and the Pork Chop Sandwich

The 1977 Chicago White Sox team hit a total of 192 home runs, an American League record which stood until 1996. Due to their great power, the team was nicknamed "The South Side Hitmen." The South Side Hitmen Grille at U.S. Cellular Field offers hamburgers, turkey burgers, veggie burgers, chicken sandwiches, and a pork chop sandwich. One might wonder how it is possible to eat a pork chop sandwich, since a pork chop has a bone in it. The answer is that it is not really a pork chop but a pork fillet. However, pork chop sandwich seems to sound much better at a stand named South Side Hitmen.

Chicken Flautas

Mac & Cheese Bites

Strawberry Churro

Barbacoa Style

The Tex-Mex stand offers burritos with the choice of seasoned beef, chicken carnitas, or pork barbacoa. Barbacoa is a form of cooking that originated in the Caribbean. In contemporary Mexico it refers to meats slow-cooked over an open fire. Different meats are cooked barbacoa style, but pork is the most popular in the Yucatan Peninsula area of Mexico.

Tamale & Flauta Hut

The Tamale & Flauta Hut offers chicken and pork tamales and chicken and potato flautas. A flauta (also known as a taquito) is a Mexican dish consisting of a fried rolled-up tortilla with a filling. It is shaped like a flute ('flauta' is Spanish for flute). The Tamale & Flauta Hut serves its offerings with tomato, lettuce, cheese, sour cream and salsa tropiquena.

Mac & Cheese Bites

The Triple Play Café puts a new twist on macaroni and cheese. It offers Mac & Cheese Bites, triangular-shaped cakes of macaroni and cheese covered with batter and deep fried. Also available are Irish nachos (French fries covered with sour cream, cheese, chives, and bacon.) Although several American ballparks sells Irish nachos, don't plan on buying some the next time you're in Dublin. Dubliners have never heard of them.

Strawberry Churro

A churro is a fried dough pastry shaped into a grooved stick. It is sometimes referred to as a "Spanish doughnut." In Spain churros are eaten for breakfast, dipped in hot chocolate or coffee. Chicago Style Churros at U.S. Cellular Field customizes its churros by inserting a filling of chocolate cream, vanilla cream, or strawberry jelly.

CINCINNATI REDS

Great American Ball Park is located in downtown Cincinnati near the banks of the Ohio River. It is named for the Great American Insurance Group which is headquartered in Cincinnati. The stadium address is 100 Joe Nuxhall Way, named for the long-time Cincinnati broadcaster who died in 2007. Also, at the age of fifteen, he was the youngest person to ever play in the Majors.

Cheese Coney Dog

Featured Hot Dog/Sausage

At Great American Ball Park, Skyline Chili sells the Cincinnati classic Cheese Coney, a Coney Island-style hot dog topped with chili, cheddar cheese, onions and mustard. The original Skyline Chili was opened in Cincinnati in 1949 by Greek immigrant Nicholas Lambrinides. That restaurant location had a great view of the Cincinnati skyline; hence the name of the business. Lambrinides originated "Cincinnati-style chili," a regional chili characterized by the use of seasonings such as cinnamon, cloves, allspice, or chocolate. The chili is commonly served over spaghetti or hot dogs (the choice at Great American Ball Park.)

More Hot Dogs and Sausages

Kahn's is the official hot dog of the Cincinnati Reds. Elias Kahn founded a neighborhood retail meat market in Cincinnati in 1883. The American Beauty rose was chosen as Kahn's trademark and remains so to this day.

Queen City Sausage is the official sausage of the Cincinnati Reds. (Cincinnati is nicknamed the Queen City of the West.) Since the 1800s, Cincinnati's West End has been known as "Porkopolis," with over forty shops producing meat products for the rest of the nation. At the age of twelve, West End native Elmer Hensler worked in the meat business. In 1965, Hensler joined forces with spice man Alois Stadler and master sausage-maker George Nagel to create Queen City Sausage. Today Porkopolis' forty shops have been replaced by Queen City Sausage.

Marge Schott was the controversial owner of the Cincinnati Reds from 1984 to 1999. During her tenure she insisted that a basic hot dog should cost only one dollar. That tradition continues to this day. At the High 5 Grill located in a corner on the top deck, the $1 Value Dog can still be purchased. However, one should note that it does not take more than two or three bites to consume a Value Dog.

Frisch's Big Boy

Frisch's Big Boy serves hamburgers, chicken fingers, and French fries. Its hamburger comes with tartar sauce and fans can even buy an additional side order of tartar sauce. Apparently folks in

Cincinnati really like tartar sauce. Outside the stand is a statue of "Frisch's Big Boy," a lad wearing red-checked overalls. I grew up in California and commented to my wife that the statue looked just like the iconic Bob's Big Boy statue with which I was familiar. As it turns out, it is the same fellow. After the bankruptcy of Bob's Big Boy and many legal maneuvers, Frisch's Restaurants was granted the use of the Big Boy name in Ohio, Kentucky, Indiana, and Tennessee.

Montgomery Inn

In 1951 Ted and Matula Gregory opened the Montgomery Inn in nearby Montgomery, Ohio, and turned it into a barbeque restaurant. Over the next sixty years it earned a reputation as one of the best barbeque restaurants in the area. On President Obama's 52nd birthday, Speaker of the House John Boehner ordered ribs for Obama by mail from the Montgomery Inn – perhaps the greatest sign of bipartisanship in the last ten years. Although the Montgomery Inn does not have a stand at Great American Ball Park, several other stands sell its pulled pork sandwich.

Waffle Bowl Sundae

Waffle Bowl Sundae

In 1938 Carl Lindner, Sr., opened a small dairy in Norwood, Ohio. At that time, nearly all milk was home delivered. Carl, however, had a new concept: he would process milk and other dairy products and sell them at his own dairy store. It is believed that he also was one of the first to sell milk in gallon bottles instead of quarts. His original store was known as the United Dairy Farmers. Today its dairy products, including ice cream, can be found in many grocery stores. At Great American Ball Park, United Dairy Farmers sells ice cream either in a waffle cone or a waffle bowl. The ice cream is topped with chocolate or caramel sauce, peanuts, whipped cream, sprinkles, and cherries.

Goetta

At Great American Ball Park, a local specialty known as a Goetta Burger is available. Goetta is a breakfast sausage of German-American origin, popular in the Cincinnati area. Goetta is ground beef combined with steel-cut oats. The Goetta Burger is served on a pretzel bun with onions and peppers.

Goetta Burger

Crunch 'n Munch

In the Cracker Jack chapter of this book, it was noted that in 2004 the New York Yankees replaced Cracker Jack popcorn with Crunch 'n Munch, a similar concoction. A fan outcry led to the Yankees returning to Cracker Jack. Great American Ball Park is now selling Crunch 'n Munch instead of Cracker Jack. So far I have not heard of any fan uprising.

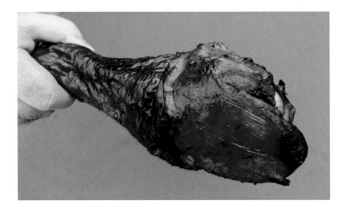

Smoked Turkey Leg

Mr. Red's Smokehouse

Barbeque is served at Mr. Red's Smokehouse. Daily offerings include a smoked prime rib sandwich, a smoked turkey leg, a smoked pulled pork sandwich, and smoked chicken wings. There was also a specialty item for each of the Reds 26 homestands during the 2014 season. On the day we visited, the homestand special was a smoked salmon burger made from ground Atlantic salmon blended with chipotle aioli. Also available is Mr. Red's version of nachos known as The Chipper. The Chipper uses homemade potato chips instead of the usual tortilla chips. The chips are topped with pulled pork, cheese sauce, barbeque sauce, onions, red and green bell peppers, and jalapeños.

The Chipper

CLEVELAND INDIANS

Progressive Field, which opened in 1994, is in downtown Cleveland. From 1994 to 2008 it was known as Jacobs Field after team owners Richard and David Jacobs. It was ranked as major league baseball's best ballpark in a 2008 *Sports Illustrated* fan poll.

Featured Hot Dog/Sausage

The C Dawg is a one-half pound all-beef hot dog, butterflied and grilled, and topped with chili, diced onions, and shredded cheddar cheese. It is advertised as "the hot dog you eat with a knife and fork." The spelling of "dawg" probably comes from the bleacher section at the nearby Cleveland Browns football stadium, which their fans call "The Dawg Pound."

C Dawg

More Hot Dogs and Sausages

Also available at the C Dawg stand is a Super Italian Sausage or a Super Bratwurst. Fans can choose any four toppings from a list of either hot or cold items. Hot toppings available are chili, bacon bits, pulled pork, peppers and onions, sauerkraut, and baked beans. Cold toppings include shredded cheddar cheese, cole slaw, diced onions, Fritos, and barbeque sauce.

Hometown Sausages sells an Italian sausage, a spicy Cajun sausage, and a broccoli and cheddar sausage where ground-up broccoli is mixed with the meat.

In Cleveland, the great debate is not about which hot dog to have, but rather which mustard to choose. The two rival brands are Stadium Mustard and Bertman Original Ballpark Mustard. Both mustards have a distinctive spicy, tangy taste and are a special color of brown. Stadium Mustard is the official mustard of Progressive Field.

Kosher hot dogs and sausages are available at a kosher stand, but the day we visited, though open for business, a posted sign read "This stand is not kosher-certified today." This reminds me of the joke: What do you call a fly without any wings? Answer: a walk.

Veggie Burger

The Burgers and Fries stand sells cheeseburgers, hamburgers, grilled chicken sandwiches, chicken

Veggie Burger

Sweet and Salty Chipper

tenders, French fries, and veggie burgers. Although veggie burgers are popular today, the first commercially sold veggie burger appeared just 32 years ago. Gregory Sams, owner of a vegetarian restaurant in London, experimented with a variety of ingredients to come up with the "VegeBurger" patty that was sold dry and needed to be rehydrated before being cooked. The VegeBurgers were sold under the brand name of Harmony Foods. Over time, in the United States, "vege" became "veggie." The veggie burgers at Progressive Field are made from black beans and corn.

The Chipper

The Chipper displays its offerings as "Our spin on the loaded nacho using house made kettle chips fried fresh daily." The variations on the Chipper include three meat-centric items (the CleOH, the BBQ and the Mexican) and one dessert offering (the Sweet and Salty.) The CleOH has chunks of corned beef and a cheese sauce, covered with pico de gallo, jalapeños, scallions, and sour cream. The BBQ replaces the corned beef with chunks of pulled pork and adds barbeque sauce. The Mexican uses seasoned ground beef in place of the corned beef. The Chipper also sells The Sweet and Salty. Chocolate and caramel sauce are drizzled on top of the kettle chips, with a side of whipped cream for dipping. According to 2013 article on the *Good Housekeeping* website, sweet and savory is one of the "five hottest trends in snack foods."

Spuds

Spuds and Suds sells fresh-cut fries and garlic fries. Customers can watch the process from whole fresh potatoes being sliced and then fried. Perhaps you haven't, but I have always wondered why potatoes are called "spuds." Research has uncovered a story as interesting as Harry M. Stevens and the origin of the hot dog in America. A commonly cited legend claims there was a nineteenth-century activist group called The Society for the Prevention of an Unwholesome Diet (SPUD), which was formed to keep potatoes out of Britain. Well-known linguist Mario Andrew Pei wrote a bestseller in 1949 entitled *The Story of Language,* in which he passed on the SPUD story. However, according to linguist David Wilton, there is no evidence that the practice of pronouncing acronyms began before the twentieth century. Another theory states that a spade used to dig up large rooted plants (such as potatoes) was known in the mid-nineteenth century as a "spud." Like the origin of the hot dog, no one knows for sure.

Fried Cookie Dough

Fried Delights sells funnel cake, corn dogs, and fried chocolate chip cookie dough. Raw cookie dough is deep fried, similar to the concept of deep-fried Twinkies.

Pierre's Ice Cream

Pierre's Ice Cream Shop opened in 1932 in Cleveland at the corner of East 82nd Street and Euclid Avenue. Alexander Pierre Basset manufactured the ice cream in the back of his shop. The company has expanded throughout the years, but each time it built a new facility, it has been located within three miles of the original shop. In 2011 Pierre's opened a 35,000-square-foot factory located one mile west of the original shop. At Progressive Field, Pierre's sells soft serve as well as hard dip ice cream. Flavors include strawberry chip, mint chocolate chip, cookie dough, and moose tracks (fudge ripple ice cream filled with crushed peanut butter cups).

Fried Chocolate Chip Cookie Dough

COLORADO ROCKIES

Coors Field opened in 1995 in downtown Denver. One of the first names considered for the new stadium was "Jurassic Park" because of the seven-foot-long triceratops skull found on the site during construction. This led to the selection of a dinosaur as the Rockies mascot, "Dinger." Denver's reputation as "the mile-high city" is noted by the twentieth row of seats in the upper deck being a different color, marking the one-mile elevation.

Elk Bratwurst

Featured Hot Dog/Sausage

At most ballparks, fan choices for hot dogs and sausages are either beef, pork, or vegetarian. At Coors Field buffalo dogs and elk bratwurst are available. The elk bratwurst (known as "Elk Brat") comes with grilled onions and peppers. According to the North American Elk Breeders Association, elk meat is high in protein and low in fat, cholesterol and calories compared to beef.

More Hot Dogs and Sausages

As the name of the stand implies, Sausage on a Stick serves (you guessed it!) sausages on a stick similar to the way corn dogs are served. The varieties are Cheddarwurst, Spicy Polish, and Sweet Italian. The sausages are provided by the Gold Star Sausage Company of Denver, a family-owned and operated business since 1936 and the largest purveyor of sausages in the Rocky Mountain region.

At Xtreme Dogs fans can choose from six varieties of gourmet hot dogs. The Denver Dog comes with "stinkin'" green chili, shredded cheddar cheese, and jalapeños. The Diablo Dog has red chili, diced red onions, shredded pepper jack cheese and jalapeños. The New York Dog has sauerkraut, spicy brown mustard, diced onions, and sliced peppers. The Santa Fe Dog has sour cream, red chili, shredded cheddar cheese, and jalapeños. The Chicago Dog has relish, diced onions, sport peppers, wedge tomatoes, cucumbers, and celery salt. Finally, the Bacon Blue Dog has blue cheese, diced onions, and bacon.

Chocolate Bacon

Famous Dave's and Chocolate Bacon

Barbeque lovers can enjoy a variety of food items at the Famous Dave's stand at Coors Field. Dave Anderson, the founder of this nationally known pit barbeque restaurant chain, did not do well academically in high school. But he had a dream to "create the best BBQ America ever tasted." Author and motivational speaker Zig Zigler dedicated his *Success for Dummies* book to Famous Dave, and featured Dave's life story. In addition to St. Louis-style ribs, Texas beef brisket, and Georgia chopped pork, Famous Dave's also offers its meat in dessert format: chocolate covered bacon. Three pieces of bacon dipped in melted milk chocolate are served chilled.

#17 Helton Burger Shack

The #17 Helton Burger Shack is named for former Colorado Rockies infielder Todd Helton, who not only wore the number 17 on his uniform but played his entire 17-year major league career with the Rockies. The Helton Burger is served with white American cheese, Thousand Island dressing, pickles and onions. Also available are fresh-cut fries and jumbo onion rings.

Rocky Mountain Oysters

With Coors Field being located in the Rocky Mountains, it is no surprise that Rocky Mountain Oysters are sold at the Blake Street Grill. Rocky Mountain oysters are not really oysters, but bull calf testicles coated in flour, pepper and salt, and then deep-fat fried. They are served with cocktail sauce. Rocky Mountain Oysters are common in cattle ranching areas of the American West, Canada, and Argentina.

Rocky Mountian Oysters

Wazee Market

The Wazee Market features three meaty sandwich creations. The Pretzel Pastrami Sandwich is made with pastrami, Swiss cheese and sauerkraut on a pretzel roll. The Smoked Brisket Bacon Melt is grilled and includes brisket, bacon, and Swiss cheese. The Rocky Mountain Ribeye Steak Sandwich is topped with cheddar cheese and fried onion rings. Meat and potato lovers can also order loaded tots to accompany their sandwiches. The tots are topped with bacon, green onions, sour cream, and cheese.

Loaded Tater Tots

Infield Greens

Infield Greens advertises "fresh salads built your way." Fans create their own salads in four steps: (1) Choose your green: spinach, romaine, iceberg, or spring mix; (2) Add a protein: chicken, shrimp, or tofu; (3) Choose up to five toppings from the more than a dozen available; (4) Top it with one of six dressings. Some of the ingredients may come from the sustainable herb and vegetable garden initiated near Gate A at Coors Field in 2013, where produce is grown on site.

Berrie Kabob

Berrie Kabobs

Fruit and chocolate lovers will be satisfied with the dessert at The Original Berrie Kabobs. Chunks of bananas and whole strawberries are skewered and then drizzled with white and dark chocolate. The stand also serves frozen cheesecake, dipped in milk chocolate, on a stick.

DETROIT TIGERS

Comerica Park opened in 2000 in the Grand Circus Park neighborhood of Detroit. The entrance to the stadium is adorned with multiple bigger-than-life-size statues of tigers in various fierce poses. The carnival atmosphere continues inside the stadium, where a carousel and Ferris wheel offer rides during the baseball games.

Featured Hot Dog/Sausage

The hot dog stand inside the Big Cat Food Court offers the Late Night Dog. The hot dog is topped with a fried egg, bacon bits, and shredded cheese (the perfect snack when the Tigers night game goes into the 18th inning).

Late Night Dog

More Hot Dogs and Sausages

Five other specialty dogs are available within the Big Cat Food Court. The Frank N' Beans Dog is topped with baked beans, shredded cheese, and bacon bits. The Coney Dog is topped with Coney sauce and onions. Detroit Coney sauce is an all-meat no-bean chili with onions and yellow mustard. The recipe does not come from Coney Island, New York, but rather from the American Coney Island restaurant in Detroit. The restaurant was founded in 1907 by Greek immigrant (by way of New York's Ellis Island) Gust Keros.

The Slaw Dog is a Coney Dog that adds cole slaw to the topping. The Chicago Dog is topped with relish, pickles, peppers, tomatoes, onions, and celery salt. Finally, the Poutine Dog is topped with French fries, gravy, and cheese curds. Poutine is a popular Canadian dish, and for those geograph-ically challenged readers, Detroit is only two miles from Windsor, Ontario, Canada. Windsor is actually south of Detroit, but this is probably more geography than you wanted to know.

Each of the specialty dogs are advertised as coming with "a natural casing." Natural casings are edible, derived from the intestinal tract of farmed animals (yum). Natural casings breathe and allow cooking flavors to infuse the meat.

Throughout the park, carts sell Winter's Italian sausages and kosher hot dogs. Winter Sausage Manufacturing Company, located in nearby Eastpointe, was founded in 1951 by Eugene Winter, a master sausage maker from Germany. The company is managed today by Eugene's daughter, Rose Mary Wuerz.

Hot dogs at Comerica Park are provided by Ball Park Franks. In 1959 Hygrade Food Products became the exclusive supplier of hot dogs at the Detroit Tigers stadium. The company sponsored a contest to come up with a name for the hot dogs, and Mary Ann Kurk won the contest with the name "Ball Park Franks." Her prize was a leather living room chair and $25 in cash. Since then, Hy-grade Food Products has been sold to Hanson Industries, who then sold it to Sara Lee Corporation, who transferred the product to its Hillshire Farms brand, who then sold it to Tyson Foods.

Salsa

At Comerica Park, nachos are all about the salsa. Jack and Annette Aronson started making fresh all-natural salsa at their small restaurant in nearby Ferndale. The owner of an upscale grocery chain tried some and was so impressed that he asked them to package it for his stores. Fifteen years later, their Garden Fresh Gourmet salsa is the country's number one selling refrigerated salsa. Food manufacturers no longer need to hire high-priced consultants to write a mission statement, as they can just copy the Aronson's. "Gather the world's best ingredients, craft them into delicious, high-quality, proprietary products and offer them at a reasonable price." At this point it is probably anticlimactic, but in addition to Garden Fresh Gourmet salsa, the nachos grande at Comerica Park are topped with all the usual nacho ingredients.

"Pizza! Pizza!"

When ballpark pizza is sold by a large national chain, I have not included it in this book. An exception is made for Comerica Park, because Little Caesar's pizza originated in Garden City, Michigan, near Detroit. Mike and Marian Ilitch invested their $10,000 life savings to open the first Little Caesar's in 1959. Today Little Caesar's is the largest carry-out pizza chain in the world, and Mike Ilitch, once a minor-league player for the Tigers, owns the Detroit Tigers as well as the Detroit Red Wings of the National Hockey League. At Comerica Park, fans can get cheese, pepperoni, the three-meat treat (sausage, bacon, pepperoni), or classic veggie (onion, green pepper, mushroom).

Hudsonville Creamery

Hudsonville Creamery started making ice cream in 1926 in Holland, Michigan, on the shore of Lake Michigan. The initial flavors in 1926 were vanilla, chocolate, strawberry, butter pecan, orange pineapple, and tootie fruitie. The Creamery is still family owned. Flavors available at Comerica Park include Tiger Traxx and Grand Traverse Bay. Tiger Traxx is cherry vanilla ice cream loaded with chocolate covered pretzels shaped as baseballs and finished with a thick fudge swirl. Traverse City, located in the Traverse Bay region of Michigan, claims to be the "cherry capital of the world." Grand Traverse Bay ice cream is amaretto flavored with cherry pieces and a thick fudge swirl.

Bumpy Cake

Sanders Chocolates was opened in Detroit by Fred Sanders in 1875. Although none exists today, at one time there were 57 stores throughout the Great Lakes region. In 2002 the brand name was sold to Morley Candy Makers. In 1913 Sanders Chocolates had begun making what it called "Devil's Food Buttercream Cake." The chocolate layer cake was topped with thick rows of piped buttercream frosting, then covered with a fudge frosting. Although Sanders called it a "Devil's Food Buttercream Cake," families around Detroit simply knew it as "a bumpy

Bumpy Cake

cake." Although the bumpy cake sold at Comerica Park is not made by Sanders, the creation is still enjoyed today.

The Infamous Bacon Burger

Infamous Bacon Burger

The 313 Burger Company (named for Detroit's area code of 313) offers fans The Infamous Bacon Burger. Unlike other bacon burgers, which are simply hamburgers topped with bacon, the Infamous Bacon Burger's patty is made with 50% ground beef and 50% ground bacon. The burger is then topped with more bacon as well as onion rings and barbeque sauce.

313 Taco Company

The 313 Taco Company cart advertises that the company has been selling "authentic street tacos since 2014." (Hopefully this claim will be a bit more impressive a few years down the road.) The street tacos are served in corn tortillas and, in addition to the normal toppings, contain Cotija cheese. Cotija is a cow's milk cheese that comes from Cotija, Michoacan, Mexico. The cheese is salty with a taste similar to Greek feta cheese, a sheep or goat's milk product.

Elephant Ears

Side Kicks sells corn dogs, chicken fingers, and elephant ears. Chicken fingers are not the fingers of chickens, and elephant ears are not the ears of elephants. In fact, elephant ears don't even come from elephants. Elephant ears, a common carnival food, are made from dough fried in the shape of an elephant ear and covered with powdered sugar.

Hicory-Smoked Soy Riblet

Hickory-Smoked Soy Riblet

Although the Brush Fire Grill serves beef brisket, pulled pork, cheeseburgers and grilled chicken sandwiches, it also has a very large vegetarian menu. It offers a veggie dog, a veggie Italian sausage, and two types of veggie burgers (black bean or garden burger). Additionally, it has a hickory-smoked riblet sandwich made from soy which resembles the McDonald's McRib.

Bavarian Pretzel Sticks

Also available at the Brush Fire Grill are grilled Bavarian pretzel sticks. Bavarian pretzels are crunchy on the outside and soft on the inside. Legend has it that in 1839 Anton Nepomuk Pfannenbrenner, a baker for the Royal Coffee House located in Munich, was preparing sweet pretzels for his guests. Instead of brushing them with sugar water, he accidentally brushed them with a baking soda-lye solution used to clean and disinfect the bakery counter tops. The pretzels came out of the oven with a brown crust, soft center, and delicious taste. The Brush Fire Grill serves its warm Bavarian Pretzel Sticks with a cheese dipping sauce.

Bavarian Pretzel Sticks

HOUSTON ASTROS

Minute Maid Park, nicknamed The Juice Box, opened in 2000 in downtown Houston. The ballpark was originally known as Enron Field, until Enron declared bankruptcy in one of America's largest business scandals. The park has a retractable roof to protect fans and players from Houston's extremely humid weather.

Featured Hot Dog/Sausage

The Extreme Dog stand sells five regional hot dogs including the Texas Dog. The Texas Dog is wrapped in bacon, topped with jalapeño relish, and served on Texas toast. Texas toast is usually made from white bread sliced twice as thick as usual sliced bread. It is believed that Texas toast was first served at Kirby's Pig Stand restaurant in Dallas in the 1920s. It has remained a popular side dish throughout Texas.

Texas Dog

More Hot Dogs and Sausages

The other regional dogs sold at the Extreme Dog stand are the Cincinnati Cheese Coney (chili, cheddar cheese and diced onions), the Georgia Dog (creamy coleslaw, barbeque sauce and diced onions), the Coney Island Dog (chili, chopped onions and spicy mustard), and the Ken Hoffman New York City Dog (grilled sauerkraut and spicy mustard). Ken Hoffman is a food columnist for the *Houston Chronicle*. According to the *Houston Chronicle* website, "Ken has written more than 800 fast food reviews. His cholesterol is higher than yours."

The Astros Sizzling Grill serves sausages. The Grill follows the Extreme Dog in offering its sausages in the same five regional versions. Each version is available either as a mild sausage or as a jalapeño hot sausage.

Fans who want pork hot dogs or sausages are out of luck at Minute Maid Park. All hot dogs and sausages are beef and are provided by Nolan Ryan All-Natural Beef. During Nolan Ryan's 27-year major league career, he pitched for the Houston Astros and the Texas Rangers as well as the New York Mets and the California Angels. He holds the major league record with seven career no-hitters and was inducted into the National Baseball Hall of Fame in 1999. Ryan is the only major league player to have his number retired by three teams (Astros, Rangers, Angels). On his website, Nolan Ryan states "While you may know me as a baseball player, the cattle business has always been my first passion. I started raising cattle when I was very young. Even then I was just as dedicated to producing the best beef possible as I am today!" Many stands throughout the park sell Nolan Ryan's regular hot dog and jumbo foot-long hot dog, as well as his brisket sausage.

Blue Bell Creameries

Blue Bell Creameries, originally known as the Brenham Creamery Company, was founded in 1907 in Brenham, Texas (about 75 miles northwest of Houston.) The company began making ice cream in the 1920s and soon changed its name to Blue Bell Creameries, after the native Texas blue bell wildflower. Blue Bell ice cream is sold in supermarkets throughout the South. At Minute Maid Park fans can enjoy Blue Bell ice cream in the following flavors: homestyle vanilla, Dutch chocolate, cookies and cream, or birthday cake (vanilla ice cream with pieces of chocolate cake, a chocolate icing swirl and multi-colored sprinkles.)

Texas Smoke

The state of Texas is famous for its brisket. The Texas Smoke stand at Minute Maid Park offers both sliced and chopped barbeque brisket sandwiches. A cooked brisket has two parts known as "the point" and "the flat." The sliced meat comes from the flat or meaty side of the brisket; the chopped meat comes from the point or fatter side.

New York Strip Steak Sandwich

New York Strip Steak Sandwich

The Texas Legends Grill features hamburgers made with—you guessed it—Nolan Ryan's beef. In addition to a basic hamburger, the Legends Grill offers cheeseburgers, bacon cheeseburgers, and a mushroom Swiss burger. The New York Strip Steak Sandwich comes with white cheese, horseradish, and fried onions. A New York strip steak is cut from the short loin of the beef and consists of a muscle that does little work and therefore is particularly tender.

Little Bigs

The Little Bigs stand serves sliders advertised as "The best things in life are in 3." Here is one of the few places at Minute Maid Park where pork is available. The sliders, which are either hamburgers or pulled pork, are served on soft rolls. The burgers are topped with cheese and onions; the pulled pork sliders are topped with cole slaw.

Tex-Mex

The El Real Grill serves Tex-Mex food, a unique blend of traditional American and Mexican-American cuisines. The El Real Grill offers beef and

Chicken Fajitas

chicken fajitas. Fans can watch the fresh tortillas being patted out and run through the machine as they wait for their order.

Chicken Caesar Salad

Green Fork

The Green Fork serves four fresh salads. The Taco Salad has iceberg lettuce, chick peas, roasted corn, black beans, red onion, spicy French dressing, and taco meat served in a tortilla shell. The Astros Signature Caesar has romaine lettuce, Caesar dressing, croutons, and Parmesan cheese. The Texas Cobb has iceberg lettuce, blue cheese, tomatoes, cucumbers, eggs, olives, bacon, avocados, and blue cheese dressing. The Heart Healthy Salad has spinach, bell peppers, cucumbers, carrots, cilantro, grape tomatoes, avocados, red onions, and balsamic dressing. All salads can be topped with grilled chicken or taco meat, if desired.

Street Eats

"Houston's hot and local" Street Eats is based on the food truck concept. The Texas chuckwagon is considered a precursor to the American food truck. At Street Eats fans can get lobster rolls, pulled pork tacos, smoked pork sandwiches, or the Texas Hold'em Sandwich (named for the popular poker game.) The Texas Hold'em has barbequed chicken, cheddar cheese, tomato, jalapeños, and cole slaw piled on Texas toast.

KANSAS CITY ROYALS

Kauffman Stadium, originally called Royals Stadium, opened in 1973. A major stadium renovation took place from 2007 to 2009. The stadium is named for Ewing Kauffman, the original owner of the Royals. Kauffman Stadium is part of the Harry S Truman Sports Complex along with Arrowhead Stadium, home of the Kansas City Chiefs football team.

Featured Hot Dog/Sausage

The Dugout Dog House offers seven specialty dogs. Since Kansas City is well known for its barbeque, the All-Star BBQ Dog is our featured hot dog. It comes with pulled pork, cole slaw, pickles, and barbeque sauce.

All-Star BBQ Dog

More Hot Dogs and Sausages

At the Dugout Dog House, the Kansas City Dog has Swiss cheese, grilled sauerkraut and Boulevard Pale Ale Mustard. Boulevard is the best-selling craft beer in the Midwest. The Blazing Buffalo Dog has pulled chicken tossed in spicy buffalo sauce and topped with cole slaw. The Royal Bacon Blue Dog has blue cheese crumbles, chopped bacon, and red onion.

Three of the hot dogs at Dugout Dog House are named for other areas of the country. The Texas Dog has chili, cheddar cheese, diced onions, and Frito bits. The New York City Dog has sauerkraut and spicy mustard and is served on a poppy seed bun. The Chicago Dog has mustard, onions, sport peppers, tomatoes, pickles, celery salt and relish.

Crown Classics sells a foot-long Sheboygan bratwurst. Bratwurst is believed to have originated in Nuremberg, Germany, and is very popular in Wisconsin. The city of Sheboygan is known as the "Bratwurst capital of the world" and celebrates Sheboygan Bratwurst Days each August.

Burnt Ends

Kansas City Barbeque

When most people think of Kansas City, barbeque comes to mind. In the early 1920s Henry Perry, known as "The Father of Kansas City Barbeque," moved to a barn on Highland Street and started barbecuing in an outdoor pit. Perry served slabs of barbequed meat wrapped in newspaper. Perry's disciples include Arthur Bryant, George Gates, Otis Boyd, John Harris, and Sherman Thompson. They all learned Perry's technique and then went on to create their own unique blends of Kansas City barbeque. Kansas City-style barbeque is slow-smoked over wood, usually hickory.

Kauffman Stadium has its own barbeque pit located behind right field. Using oak and hickory wood from the Ozarks, Kauffman's smoker produces up to 400 pounds of smoked meat on busy days. The barbeque is served at Sweet Baby Ray's. Sweet Baby Ray's is a Chicago-based company that sells its barbeque sauces and meats in grocery stores throughout the United States.

Sweet Baby Ray's serves barbeque sandwiches of ham, brisket, turkey or pulled pork, in addition to chopped burnt ends or ribs. Burnt ends are a traditional part of Kansas City barbeque. The entire brisket is cooked whole, then the point end is removed and cooked further. The longer cooking time gives rise to the name "burnt ends." A proper burnt end should display a small amount of charred meat on at least one side. The burnt ends are served either in a sandwich or in a basket with a skewer.

Cheesy Corn

In addition to the usual cole slaw, baked beans, and potato salad sides, Sweet Baby Ray's has a Kansas City specialty of cheesy corn. Cheesy corn is kernels of sweet corn served in a cheddar cheese sauce with ham and bacon bits. (Unlike cheese grits, the dish is known as "cheesy corn" and not "cheese corn." In the 2012 presidential campaign Mitt Romney, in trying to show his Southern side, said how much he liked cheesy grits. However, in the South, cheesy grits are bad grits and cheese grits are grits with cheese.)

Cheesy Corn

Belfonte Dairy

The Belfonte Ice Cream Shop is an air-conditioned indoor ice cream stand. On warm days fans seem to go there not only for ice cream, but to stay cool. Sal Belfonte, a door-to-door milkman for many years, started Belfonte Dairy as a family business. Today Belfonte ice cream is found in over 500 supermarkets and restaurants in Kansas City and surrounding areas. At Kauffman Stadium, Belfonte offers twelve "scoopilishish" flavors (including strawberry cheesecake and cookies and cream) and eight toppings.

Ice Cream with Sprinkles

Brisket-acho

Cheesy Corn Brisket-acho is Kauffman Stadium's version of nachos. Brisket, baked beans, cheesy corn, and cole slaw are piled high over a bed of chips and then topped with plenty of barbeque sauce.

Royal Bacon Blue Fries

Unlike with traditional nachos, you will need a fork to eat a Cheesy Corn Brisket-acho.

Royal Bacon Blue Fries

The Fry Works sells four version of what it calls "Extreme Fries": BBQ Pulled Pork Fries, Chili Cheese Fries, Buffalo Ranch Fries, and Royal Bacon Blue Fries. The Royal Bacon Blue Fries contain bacon, ranch dressing, blue cheese and green onions.

Nutty Bavarian

The Nutty Bavarian offers almonds, cashews, pecans, and peanuts coated with sugar and cinnamon. Fans can watch the nuts swirling around in the coating machine while the sugar and cinnamon are added.

LOS ANGELES ANGELS OF ANAHEIM

Angel Stadium of Anaheim opened in 1966, located within several miles of Disneyland. In front of the stadium is the landmark "Big A" sign and electronic marquee. The halo located near the top of the 230-foot tall, 210-ton sign is illuminated following games the Angels win, which gives rise to the fan expression, "Light up the Halo!"

Featured Hot Dog/Sausage

For many years the signature hot dog at Angel Stadium was the Halo Dog (an all-beef hot dog wrapped with bacon and topped with charro beans, shredded Monterey Jack cheese, and pico de gallo salsa). In 2014 it has been replaced by the Farmer John Jumbo Hot Dog.

Farmer John Hot Dog

Farmer John hot dogs have a history in Southern California dating back to 1931. The company claims that its product is "seasoned with every culture in the world," as represented by the population of Southern California. Farmer John hot dogs have been sold at sporting and other entertainment venues across the state, including the famous Dodger Dog at Dodger Stadium. At Angel Stadium the Jumbo Hot Dog comes "undressed" and fans can add their own condiments. It is sold at Farmer John Grilling Stations along with bratwurst, Italian sausages, and hot links.

Oggi's Pizza

Oggi's Pizza and Brewing Company serves slices of pepperoni and cheese pizza at Angel Stadium. "Oggi" is Italian for "today," chosen to represent the fresh quality of the ingredients chosen by George and John Hadjis when they opened their first restaurant in Del Mar, California. The brothers, who had formerly worked in the technology industry, expanded their sports-themed operation into a microbrewery in 1995. A few years later it was named the Champion Small Brewing Company at the World Beer Cup.

Chronic Tacos

The first Chronic Tacos location opened in Newport Beach in 2002. Here one can get Mexican street tacos (served on a soft tortilla rather than in a fried shell) with a choice of marinated grilled chicken or steak, slow-cooked pork, or all-veggie. Chronic Tacos is well known for its pork nachos. The chips

Chicken Tacos

BBQ Brisket Sandwich

Grilled Cheese Sandwich with Tomato Soup

are topped with pork, melted cheese sauce, shredded jack and cheddar cheese, rice, beans, onions, cilantro, and jalapeños.

Smoke Ring BBQ

The Smoke Ring BBQ features a variety of meats cooked over an open flame. Along with a smoked barbeque brisket sandwich, fans can order smoked half chicken, smoked kielbasa link, or St. Louis pork ribs. Side dishes include cole slaw, macaroni and cheese, and cornbread.

The Big Cheese

The Big Cheese stand offers four varieties of grilled cheese sandwiches. In addition to the traditional, fans can order thick-cut bacon, short rib, or tomato and arugula. The cheese is a mixture of cheddar and Monterey Jack. Grilled cheese sandwiches and tomato soup are often considered classic comfort food. In fact, there is a Midwest restaurant chain named Tom+Chee that specializes in this combo. Here at Angel Stadium The Big Cheese sells tomato soup to accompany any of its grilled cheese sandwiches.

Carne Asada Waffle Fries

Spuds is the place for those who like their French fries out of the ordinary. The Carne Asada Waffle Fries come with beef covered with sour cream, guacamole, jalapeños, and pico de gallo. Chili Cheese Fries are topped with short rib chili, and house-made-beer cheese. And for those who prefer sweet instead of savory, there are the Sweet Potato Fries with cinnamon and sugar.

Carne Asada Waffle Fries

LOS ANGELES DODGERS

Dodger Stadium, which opened in 1962, is the third oldest of the major league stadiums, following Fenway Park (1912) and Wrigley Field (1914). With seating for 56,000 fans, Dodger Stadium can accommodate more attendees then any other major league stadium.

Unlike most other stadiums today, Dodger Stadium does not have stands from local area merchants. At one time my favorite deli (and in my opinion, the best Jewish deli west of New York), Canter's Deli, had a stand at Dodger Stadium. It closed in 2010. Fortunately, deli fans can visit Canter's Deli on nearby Fairfax Avenue in Los Angeles before or after any Dodgers game since it is open 24 hours a day. Additionally, fans at Dodger Stadium are allowed access only to the level where their seats are located and cannot patronize food stands on other levels.

Featured Hot Dog/Sausage

Harry M. Stevens would be pleased to know that nearly every concession stand at Dodger Stadium offers hot dogs. The well-known Dodger Dog, a pork wiener, is available either steamed or grilled. In addition to the traditional Dodger Dog, fans can choose an all-beef Super Dodger Dog, or a Brooklyn Dodger Dog, which is all beef with a thicker casing.

Dodger Dog

Along with the Fenway Frank, the Dodger Dog is the best-known ballpark hot dog. The Dodger Dog is ten inches long (though sometimes referred to as a foot-long) and sticks out at both ends of the bun. Thomas Arthur, food concessions manager at Dodger Stadium from 1962 to 1991, created the concept of the Dodger Dog. He coined the name "Dodger Dog" after being criticized for calling it a "foot-long dog" when it was actually only ten inches long. Dodger Dogs were originally made by the Morrell Meat Company, but are now made by Farmer John, which was purchased by Hormel in 2004.

More Hot Dogs and Sausages

For fans who want a non-traditional hot dog, the Extreme Loaded Dogs stand has five varieties from which to choose. The Doyer Dog Jr., named for the Spanish pronunciation of "Dodgers," comes with chili, nacho cheese, jalapeños, and pico de gallo. LA's Extreme Bacon-Wrapped Dog is a one-third pound all-beef hot dog wrapped with three slices of applewood-smoked bacon, smothered with grilled peppers and topped with onions. During each Dodger homestand, the Extreme Loaded Dogs stand offers a special dog. When we were there, the specialty hot dog was topped with French fries and cole slaw. Extreme Loaded Dogs features not only one but two varieties of hot dogs topped with Frito corn chips. The Frito Pie Dog has chili, cheese, and Fritos. The Big Kid Dog comes topped with gooey mac and cheese and Fritos.

Pasta Platter

Pistachio Gelato

Elote

Tommy Lasorda's Trattoria

New to Dodger Stadium in 2014 is the Tommy Lasorda Trattoria, an informal Italian eatery. Tommy Lasorda was best known as a Hall-of-Fame manager of the Dodgers from 1976 to 1996. He was also known for his love of Italian food. At the stand named for Tommy Lasorda, Italian specialties include the Italian Meatball Marinara Sandwich, the Chicken Parmesan Sandwich, and the Lasorda's Pasta Platter.

The Italian Meatball Marinara Sandwich is made with hand-formed all-beef meatballs with Italian seasonings. The Chicken Parmesan Sandwich is a breaded chicken breast with provolone, grated Parmesan, and zesty marinara sauce, served on a toasted Italian roll. The Pasta Platter has penne pasta with zesty marinara sauce, Italian beef meatballs and Parmesan cheese. Also available at the Trattoria are cheese and pepperoni pizza and garlic fries smothered with a fresh garlic marinade.

Gelato, described at Tommy Lasorda's Trattoria as "Italy's original ice cream," is sold in unique flavors. The day we were there, flavors offered were cappuccino crunch, white chocolate raspberry swirl, pistachio, and panna cotta (an Italian dessert made with cream, milk, sugar and gelatin).

Elote

The Think Blue Bar-B-Que (named for the blue color of the Dodger uniform) provides barbeque beef sandwiches and Louisiana hot sausages. Also available is a Mexican-style corn on the cob known as elote. The ear of corn is roasted and seasoned with lemon, mayonnaise, Parmesan, and powdered barbeque seasonings.

Chef Merito

The L.A. Taqueria stand features Chef Merito seasonings, "the Official Seasoning of the Los

Angeles Dodgers" according to the Chef Merito website. The Taqueria serves street-style tacos with a choice of carne asada or fish, as well as chicken taquitos (a small rolled-up tortilla filled with chicken and deep fried).

Elysian Park Grill

Elysian Park is the second largest park in the city of Los Angeles and encompasses the Dodger Stadium area. It was perhaps named after Elysian Fields in Hoboken, New Jersey, the site of the first organized baseball game in 1845. The Elysian Park Grill at Dodger Stadium offers two hamburger specialties. The Dodger "Blue Heaven" Burger is a one-third pound premium burger with crumbled blue cheese, caramelized onions, and sliced tomatoes topped with a pasilla chili and chipotle aioli on a bun. The Elysian Park Cheeseburger comes with American cheese, caramelized onions, dill pickles and special dressing.

Cool-A-Coo Ice Cream Sandwich

Long a favorite with Dodger fans, the Cool-A-Coo ice cream sandwich is once again available at Dodger Stadium after an absence of more than ten years. Made in Southern California, the Cool-A-Coo features vanilla ice cream between two oatmeal cookies, dipped in a chocolate coating.

MIAMI MARLINS

Marlins Park opened in 2012 on the site of the former Miami Orange Bowl. It is located in the Little Havana section of Miami, about two miles from city center. The stadium, with its retractable roof, was rated by the U.S. Green Building Council as the greenest major league ballpark.

Pizza Dog

Ceviche

Featured Hot Dog/Sausage

Each Marlins game features a "hot dog specialty of the game." On the day we visited, the specialty dog was topped with pizza sauce, tomatoes, mozzarella cheese, mushrooms, and chopped sausage.

More Hot Dogs and Sausages

Hot dogs and sausages play a lesser role in the food offerings at Marlins Park than at many major league stadiums. The hot dogs are made by Kayem Foods which makes the famous Fenway Franks in Boston. Here Kayem provides a traditional hot dog, a chili cheese dog, and an Italian sausage.

Ceviche

Cuban and Latin American specialties are found in the section of Marlins Park called Taste of Miami. Don Camaron Seafood Grill & Market, a Miami restaurant, has a stand here. It offers a snapper sandwich, fried shrimp basket, half-dozen oysters, ceviche, conch fritters, and malanga chips.

Ceviche is a seafood dish popular in the coastal regions of Central and South America. It is made from fresh raw fish cured in citrus juices. The ceviche at Don Camaron is made with sea bass and includes sweet potatoes, Peruvian corn kernels, cilantro, onions and lime juice. Conchs are marine gastropod mollusks. The meat of conchs is eaten raw in salads or (as at Marlins Park) cooked as fritters, breaded and fried. Malanga is a root vegetable from the tropics of South America. It has been grown commercially in South Florida since 1963 to meet the demands of Latin Americans living in the region. Malanga chips take the place of potato chips at Don Camaron.

Papo Llega y Pon

The original Papo Llega y Pon was opened by retired Cuban boxer Miguel Alfonso in Miami. In Cuba, a "llega y pon" is a place where country folk would come to town and set up food for sale, often in a ramshackle hut. It has long been a favorite place for Miamians and has been favorably reviewed by food critics. Miguel's daughter Julia now runs Papo Llega y Pon. She was convinced by several Marlins employees to open a stand at Marlins Park. The featured item at Marlins Park is the roasted pork sandwich made from pork shoulder layered with extra crispy skin, salt, onions, mojo marinade, and hot sauce.

Tequenos and Empanadas

Also in the Taste of Miami section is Panna Café Express. Panna Café Express serves authentic Latin American cuisine at several locations throughout the Miami area. At Marlins Park it offers tequeños (a spear of bread dough with a white cheese filling) and empanadas (a turnover-shaped pastry with a filling of chicken or beef). The empanadas are served with aji sauce, a spicy mixture containing tomatoes, cilantro, aji peppers, and onions.

Chicken Empanadas

Goya Latin Café

Founded in 1936, Goya Foods is America's largest Hispanic-American owned food company. It sells over 2,000 food products from the Caribbean, Mexico, Spain, and parts of Central and South America. The Goya Latin Café at Marlins Park offers a pressed Cuban sandwich. Instead of the Cuban sandwich being on a roll, it is on pressed bread similar to a panini. The Café also has a veggie burger described as "a home-made black bean, maduros and yellow rice patty with shredded cabbage, sliced tomato, and chipotle aioli." Maduros are sweet, ripe plantains.

Black Bean Burger

Latin American Grill

The Latin American Grill serves Cuban sandwiches (layers of ham, pork, cheese, pickles and mustard on a grilled roll). It also has a Midnight Sandwich, which is a Cuban sandwich on a sweet roll. The sandwiches come with a side of plantain chips. Plantain is a banana-like fruit that grows in the tropics.

Kosher Korner

The Kosher Korner serves pastrami sandwiches, hot dogs, hamburgers, and cheeseburgers with soy cheese (kosher dietary laws do not allow for dairy to be mixed with meat.) Also available are fried potato knishes from Gabila's of New York, the same manufacturer of knishes sold at the Mets Citi Field.

Meatball Marinara Fries

Burger 305 offers an Italian twist on French fries with its Meatball Marinara Fries. Fried potatoes are topped with meatballs and marinara sauce.

SoBe Fruit Salad

SoBe is the nickname for the South Beach neighborhood in the city of Miami Beach. The SoBe fruit salad contains fresh local fruits (grapefruit, watermelon, pineapple, mango) plus cucumbers and yellow pear tomatoes. The salad is accompanied by a sweet pineapple-based dressing.

MILWAUKEE BREWERS

Miller Park, which opened in 2001, features major league baseball's only fan-shaped retractable roof, which allows for opening or closing in less than ten minutes. Large panes of glass allow for natural grass to grow inside the stadium.

Featured Hot Dog/Sausage

South Paw Dogs offers fans The Beast, a grilled foot-long bratwurst stuffed with a hot dog and wrapped in bacon. It is topped with beer-braised onions and sauerkraut, stadium sauce and mustard, and served on a pretzel bun. The hot dog is very narrow, which allows for it to be inserted inside the bratwurst.

The Beast

More Hot Dogs and Sausages

Fans not quite up to The Beast can get either the Milwaukee Dog or the Crab Mac n' Cheese Polish. The Milwaukee Dog is topped with bacon strips and bits, Bernie's Barrelman Ale cheese sauce, and fried cheese curds. Bernie's Barrelman Ale is the name for a new beer that celebrates the partnership between the Milwaukee Brewers and the Leinenkugel Brewing Company. The limited-release beer is available exclusively at Miller Park.

The Crab Mac n' Cheese Polish is a Polish sausage topped with crab meat, macaroni and cheese, and sriracha mayonnaise and served on a pretzel bun.

Klement's Sausage Company is the official provider at Miller Park for both the sausages and hot dogs. In addition to Polish sausages and bratwurst, fans can purchase a chorizo sausage or a cheddar bratwurst. Hot dogs come in both jumbo and junior sizes. The brothers John, George and Ron Klement opened a small sausage company in Milwaukee's South Side in 1956. Their goal was to bring "the taste of the Old Country" to the people of Milwaukee. Klement's has grown to become Milwaukee's largest producer of sausage products. In 2005 the brothers were inducted into the Wisconsin Meat Industry Hall of Fame. Although it's not quite the same as making it at Cooperstown, note that the first member inducted into the Wisconsin Meat Industry Hall of Fame was Oscar Mayer (the Babe Ruth of the Wisconsin meat industry.)

Sargento Cheese Company

Milwaukee is known for beer, sausages, and cheese. This book does not cover beer; we already talked about sausages; now it's time for the cheese. The BBQ and Burgers stand features a cheddar burger made with cheese from the Sargento Cheese Company. The Sargento Cheese Company began as the Plymouth Cheese Counter, a small delicatessen located in Plymouth, about 50 miles north of Milwaukee. Its initial product line included mozzarella, provolone, and romano cheeses. The company name comes from a combination of the founding partners' last names, Leonard Gentine and Joseph Sartori. In 1965 Gentine bought out his partner. Nearly fifty years later, the company is run by Leonard's grandson, Louie Gentine.

Palermo's Pizza

Palermo's Pizza stand offers cheese and pepperoni slices. Palermo's story is a twist on the "local pizza parlor goes national" story. Italian immigrants Gaspare and Zina Fallucca opened a pizzeria in 1969. Several years later Palermo's was named Milwaukee's best pizza by the *Milwaukee Journal*. In addition to pizza, Palermo's also sold pizza bread based on a family recipe from Zina's relatives. A local grocer urged the Falluccas to offer frozen pizza which could be baked at home. In 1989 Palermo's revolutionized the frozen pizza industry by offering the first frozen pizza with a crust that rises while it bakes. Today Palermo's frozen products can be found in grocery stores throughout the Midwest.

Cedar Crest Ice Cream

Miller Park offers its fans Cedar Crest ice cream. Cedar Crest, located 90 miles north in Manitowoc, makes its ice cream in small batches. Its only business is ice cream and it considers itself a "craft" ice cream business (similar to a microbrewery, but for ice cream.) The company's best known flavor is Elephant Tracks chocolate ice cream with shards of peanut butter cups inserted throughout. In addition to Elephant Tracks, fans can get butter pecan, chocolate chip cookie dough, cookies and cream, and many other flavors.

Stormin' Gorman Thomas

Gorman Thomas was a designated hitter/outfielder for the Milwaukee Brewers from 1973 to 1983, plus his last major league year of 1986. During the period from 1978 to 1983 he hit more home runs than any other player in the American League. He also struck out frequently and had a low batting average. He was known as Stormin' Gorman and is considered one of the all-time fan favorites in Milwaukee. Gorman's Corner stand at Miller Park, which sells traditional ballpark fare, honors Thomas. The stand also sells jumbo kosher pickles (and I mean jumbo) which are displayed in a large jar on the counter.

Meatloaf Link

The Smokehouse serves carved sandwiches of beef brisket, turkey, and Italian roast pork. It advertises "All of our meat is smoked in-house for 12 hours." During our visit there, it offered a homestand special: meatloaf sandwich. The sandwich is made from a grilled meatloaf link with bacon chipotle catsup glaze on a hoagie bun. Since Milwaukee is the sausage capital of America, the Smokehouse decided to put the meatloaf into a sausage link.

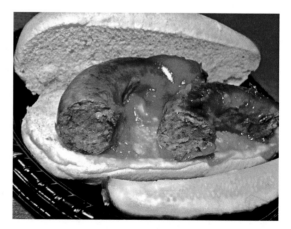

Meatloaf Link Sandwich

Walking Tacos

Texas League Tacos offers a twist on the walking taco concept. Instead of using a tortilla, the contents of the taco (beef, chicken or pork, pico de gallo, scallions and sour cream) are served inside

Spaghetti-in-a-Meatball

Fried Cheese Curd Canoe

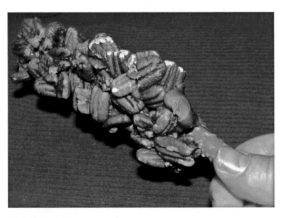

Turtle Stick

a bag of Cool Ranch Doritos. Just a hunch, but I think traditionalists may not be pleased by this offering.

Spaghetti-in-a-Meatball

The Double Clutch stand is designed to look like a food truck, saluting the food truck movement. A sign reads "Sweet eats from the street to your seat." Many places offer spaghetti and meatballs, but the Double Clutch serves Spaghetti-in-a-Meatball. A softball-sized ground beef, pork and veal meatball is stuffed with spaghetti and mozzarella cheese and topped with marinara sauce and provolone.

Fried Cheese Curd Canoe

The Home Fire Grill serves a Fried Cheese Curd Canoe. (I believe Wisconsin state law requires all businesses to sell fried cheese curds in some form.) Cheese curds are the solid parts of soured milk, sometimes referred to as "squeaky cheese." The curds squeak against the teeth when bitten into, due to air trapped inside the porous material. They have a somewhat salty, mild flavor. The fried cheese curds at the Home Fire Grill are served in a cardboard canoe-shaped box. My extensive research was not able to find a reason for the canoe shape.

Turtle Stick

The feature offering at Heavenly Roasted Nuts is the Turtle Stick. A traditional "turtle" candy (pecans in chocolate-covered caramel, shaped somewhat like a turtle) is served on a salted pretzel stick. The original turtle candy was made in 1918 by Johnson's Candy Company which later became DeMet's Candy. The turtle name was coined by an unknown candy dipper who first thought that the candy looked like a turtle.

MINNESOTA TWINS

Target Field, located in the Warehouse District near downtown Minneapolis, opened in 2010. It was designed to be a neutral park, intended to favor neither hitters nor pitchers. The park is an open-air field, creating an often chilly environment for April games.

Featured Hot Dog/Sausage

Although the scope of this book does not include beverages, we will make an exception when the beverage is advertised as "A Meal in a Cup." The Bigger Better Bloody Mary stand offers a Bloody Mary with a bratwurst on a skewer stuck into the drink. Bloody Mary is a cocktail containing vodka, tomato juice, and spices such as Worcestershire or Tabasco sauce. The cocktail ingredients give a unique flavor to the bratwurst. Both New York's 21 Club and Harry's New York Bar in Paris, France, claim to have invented the Bloody Mary.

Bloody Mary Bratwurst

More Hot Dogs and Sausages

Wasyl and Anna Kramarczuk immigrated from Ukraine in the late 1940s. Wasyl was a skilled sausage maker and Anna was an experienced baker. Together they opened Kramarczuk's Restaurant and Delicatessen in Minneapolis in 1954. Every product it sells is made by hand from scratch. At Target Field the stand sells bratwurst and Polish sausage.

Halsey's Sausage Haus is named in honor of former Twins broadcaster Halsey Hall. Hall originated the "Holy Cow!" as a home-run call long before it was used by Harry Caray. Halsey's Sausage Haus serves Italian and Polish sausages, and cheddar and plain bratwurst. The sausages are provided by the Sheboygan Sausage Company.

The hot dogs at Target Field are provided by Schweigert Meats of Minnesota. This company has a quirky website. The timeline on its website shows the first store opening in 1937. It then lists two events between 1937 and 2014. The first event is "R&D team proposes new line of specialty sausages with trendy ingredients." The second event, "Ray [Schweigert] fires R&D team." Nothing like sticking to the basics.

Murray's Restaurant

Murray's Restaurant, located several blocks from Target Field, was opened in 1946 by Art and Marie Murray. Art met Marie when she was his waitress at the Schroeder Hotel in Milwaukee. Murray's signature dish is the Silver Butter Knife Steak, purported to be so tender that it can be cut with a silver butter knife. The restaurant is still owned and operated by the Murray family. The Murray's steak sandwich is available at the Mill City Grill stand at Target Field. The sandwich is made with choice sirloin and provolone cheese, served on a ciabatta roll. Mill City Grill also serves Murray's famous garlic toast.

Andrew Zimmern of the Travel Channel

Andrew Zimmern is creator and host of the Travel Channel series *Bizarre Foods with Andrew Zimmern*. He has twice won the prestigious James Beard Foundation Award. For five years he was executive chef at the Café Un Deux Trois in Minneapolis. Andrew Zimmern's Canteen at Target Field advertises itself as "a food adventure." It offers two distinctive entrees: a Minnesota crispy belly bacon sandwich with vinegar slaw and jalapeño jelly; and a smoked meat sandwich with vinegar slaw and maple syrup hot sauce. The slice of bacon is the thickest slice of bacon I have ever seen in my life. The smoked meat is a very thinly cut brisket. Andrew Zimmern's Canteen menu literally goes "through thick and thin."

Minnesota Crispy Belly Bacon Sandwich

Turkey to Go and Ken Davis Barbeque Sauces

Turkey to Go "proudly serves turkey raised by Minnesota turkey farmers." Turkey To Go, which is owned by the Minnesota Turkey Growers Association, offers its turkey sandwich at many Minnesota festivals. At Target Field the pulled turkey sandwich is served with Ken Davis barbeque sauces. Jazz musician Ken Davis opened a barbeque restaurant in Minneapolis in the late 1960s. He spent several years trying to duplicate the barbeque sauce his grandmother had made. Once he mastered the recipe, he decided to close the restaurant and sell barbeque sauces instead. Ken died in 1991, but his barbeque sauce company is still in business.

Señor Smokes

District Del Sol is a Hispanic neighborhood of St. Paul. The first residents were migrant agricultural workers who came in the early twentieth century. The community remained small until the 1980s when many immigrants from Mexico and Central America settled in the neighborhood. El Burrito Mercado, located in District Del Sol, provides burritos and other Mexican dishes to the Señor Smokes stand at Target Field. The Señor Smokes stand offers burritos and a Walk-A-Taco (an ice-cream-cone shaped tortilla filled with traditional taco ingredients). Señor Smoke was the nickname of former Twins pitcher Juan Berenguer.

Loon Café Chili

In addition to sausages, Halsey's Sausage Haus sells chili from the Loon Café in Minneapolis. This classic Texas style chili contains cubed sirloin steak, onions, Tex-Mex spices and chili pepper. The Loon Café has been featured in magazines such as *Esquire, Rolling Stone,* and *Bon Appétit.* It is also noted as one of America's best singles bars and, according to *Playboy* magazine, the clientele includes "office workers, docs, lawyers, art folks, visiting celebs, ladies openly on the move."

Walleye and Chips

Minneapple Pie

Walleye and Chips

The State Fair Classics stand features items from three local food purveyors. Mac's Fish & Chips was opened in 1991 in St. Paul by former Minnesota North Star hockey player Tom McCarthy. At Target Field fans can get Mac's Walleye and Chips. Walleye is a freshwater fish native to Canada and the northern United States.

Pork Chop on a Stick

J.D. Hoyt's Supper Club is located several blocks from Target Field and caters to the "before and after game" crowd. During the game, fans can order Hoyt's Pork Chop on a Stick. I could try to describe it further, but the name says it all.

Minneapple Pie

The famous 1974 Chevrolet ad talked about "baseball, hot dogs, apple pie and Chevrolet." George Atsidakos has taken his Minneapple Pie to Target Field. George's parents, Andy and Libby, ran several restaurants in the Minneapolis area. George modified his father's apple pie recipe and created a deep-fried apple pie in the shape of a mini turnover. His creation became known as the Minneapple Pie, sold at fairs and festivals. Fans at Target Field can get the Minneapple Pie at the State Fair Classics stand.

Izzy's Ice Cream

Attorney Lara Hammel and her husband Jeff Sommers, a middle-school teacher, decided they wanted to open an ice cream shop. After a great deal of research, they opened Izzy's in St. Paul in 2000. In May of 2005 *Readers' Digest* named Izzy's the best ice cream shop in America. Flavors at Target Field include salted caramel, peppermint bonbon, cookies and cream, and church elder berry.

Tony Oliva

Tony Oliva played his entire 15-year career with the Minnesota Twins. He was the American League Rookie of the Year in 1964 and won several batting titles during his career. Tony grew up in Pinar del Rio, Cuba. A scout for the Minnesota Twins saw him play in Cuba and invited him to play for the Twins organization. He did not want to leave home, but his father encouraged him to "become rich and famous in America." At Target Field Tony is remembered at the Tony O's stand where Cuban sandwiches are sold. The Target Field version comes with ham, pulled pork, Swiss cheese, Dijon mustard and pickles.

Frank Viola

Frank Viola was a pitcher for the Minnesota Twins from 1982 to 1989. He was the World Series MVP in 1987 and won the American League Cy Young Award in 1988. Viola was nicknamed "Sweet Music" by a Minnesota sports writer who said when Viola pitched, there was sweet music in the dome (referring to the Metrodome, former home of the Twins.) The Italian food stand at Target Field is named Frankie V's in honor of Viola. It serves house made meatballs, calzones, and pizza from Papa John's.

Minnesota Wild Rice

Wild rice is not related to the more familiar Asian rice. The plant grows widely in shallow water in small lakes and streams in Minnesota. The grain is a steady diet for ducks and other aquatic wildlife. Several Native American cultures including the Ojibwa, consider wild rice to be a sacred plant. Target Field offers Minnesota Wild Rice Soup made with chunks of chicken and assorted vegetables. While visiting the stadium in the summer, I was able to imagine having a warming bowl on a cold April day.

Minnesota Wild Rice Soup

Rib Tip Basket

Located in the courtyard just inside the main gate of Target Field is the Butcher and the Boar stand. The flavors from its smoker greets fans as they enter the stadium. The Butcher sells a Smoke and Fire Rib Tip Basket. Rib tips are chewy strips cut from the lower ends of spareribs.

NEW YORK METS

Citi Field opened in 2009 next to the site of Shea Stadium, former home of the Mets and location of the 1964-65 World's Fair. Visitors entering Citi Field through the front entrance pass through the Jackie Robinson Rotunda, where the Brooklyn Dodgers legendary player is honored.

Featured Hot Dog/Sausage

The Hot Pastrami and Rye stand announces "We make our own hot pastrami, hand-carved and piled high on rye bread, served with deli mustard and a kosher dill pickle." For those who love New York pastrami but still believe you should have a hot dog at a ball game, there is a perfect solution: Hot Pastrami and Rye serves a Pastrami Dog. A Nathan's hot dog is covered with chopped pastrami and served in a hot dog bun.

Pastrami Dog

More Hot Dogs and Sausages

The Kosher Grill serves all-beef hot dogs as well as all-beef sweet sausages with grilled onions and peppers. Fried potato knishes from Gabila's (known as the original Coney Island square knish) are available at the Kosher Grill.

Pat LaFrieda

In 1922 Italian immigrant Anthony LaFrieda opened a butcher shop in Brooklyn. Anthony taught the business to his five sons. In 1950 they expanded to a shop in New York City's meatpacking district on West 14th Street. The shop was on the second floor of a building with no elevator and the

Meatball Sliders

LaFrieda brothers had to carry 200-pound hind saddles of beef on their backs, up a flight of stairs. Today the business, now known as Pat LaFrieda Meat Purveyors, is run by the next generation of LaFriedas. Citi Field features three stands offering Pat LaFrieda meat dishes.

Pat LaFrieda's Original Filet Mignon Steak Sandwich stand advertises, "The original LaFrieda family recipe showcases hand cut 100% Black Angus seared filet mignon, topped with Vermont Monterey Jack cheese and sweet caramelized onions served on a custom made toasted French baguette." Pat LaFrieda's Signature Meatball Sliders stand announces "A trio of Grandpa LaFrieda's all-beef meatball sliders in traditional homemade tomato sauce topped with whipped ricotta cheese served on a locally-baked toasted roll." Also available at the Pat LaFrieda's Burgers stand are classic hamburgers and cheeseburgers.

Chef Danny Meyer

New York City chef and restaurant owner Danny Meyer has opened four stands at Citi Field. Shake Shack and Blue Smoke are outposts of his restaurants; El Verano Taqueria and Box Frites are stands created for Citi Field (and also Nationals Park in Washington, DC).

Shake Shack

The Shake Shack has become one of the hottest hamburger spots in New York City. Shake Shack started as a hot dog cart in Madison Square Park. The cart was a huge success, with fans lined up daily for three summers. Since then the Shake Shack has expanded to restaurants across the Northeast U.S. and around the world. The Shake Shack stand at Citi Field offers their classic ShackBurger. Its burgers are 100% all-natural Angus beef with "no hormones and no antibiotics ever." It also serves a vegetarian 'ShroomBurger, a crisp fried portobello mushroom filled with melted Muenster and cheddar cheeses and topped with their special Shack Sauce. End your Shake Shack meal with a frozen custard, a dense and creamy ice cream spun fresh daily.

Blue Smoke

Danny Meyer envisioned opening a restaurant in New York that would bring "…the soulful cuisine of America's South and Midwest." This vision became Blue Smoke. The flagship Blue Smoke is combined with the club Jazz Standard on East 27th Street in New York City. At Citi Field fans can enjoy a North Carolina applewood-smoked pulled pork sandwich, a grilled or fried chicken sandwich with buttermilk ranch sauce, a hickory-smoked beef brisket sandwich with spicy Kansas City sauce, or smoked chipotle chicken wings. Sides include thick-cut French fries dusted with Blue Smoke "magic dust" seasoning, slow-cooked pit beans with pulled pork, vinegar-based slaw, and cornbread served with chipotle butter.

El Verano Taqueria

El Verano Taqueria offers tacos, quesadillas, burritos, and nachos. Each of these four menu items can be made with a choice of steak (char-grilled sirloin), chicken pipian (grilled chicken breast with green mole), carnitas (slow-cooked pork shoulder), or vegetarian (roasted portobello mushrooms, zucchini, corn, and poblano peppers).

Meat the Mets Pizza

Two Boots Pizza

Two Boots Pizza serves Louisiana-style Italian pizza. The name comes from the shapes of both Louisiana and Italy, which look like boots. Although Two Boots serves the usual cheese and pepperoni slices, it also serves slices not found elsewhere. The Happy Recap slice comes with homemade andouille meatballs, ricotta, mozzarella and piquant sauce on a round Sicilian crust. The Meat the Mets slice contains Creole chicken, pepperoni, sweet Italian sausage, jalapeños, ricotta and mozzarella. The V for Vegan slice comes with artichokes, shiitake mushrooms, red onions, pesto, and Daiya non-dairy cheese.

Box Frites

Box Frites (French for "chips") specializes in gourmet French fries. The thick-cut Idaho fries or sweet potato fries come with a choice of Buffalo blue cheese, smokey bacon, pesto, chipotle barbeque, or rosemary ranch dipping sauces. Also available at Box Frites are garlic fries and cheddar bacon fries, topped with crumbled Applewood-smoked bacon, cheddar sauce, and fresh scallions.

Mama's of Corona

Mama's of Corona sells hero sandwiches and salads. Its signature hero, known as Mama's Italian Special, has pepper ham, salami, homemade mozzarella, mushrooms, and peppers. The antipasto salad features salami, pepperoni, green and black olives, carrots, red cabbage, marinated mushrooms, artichoke hearts, and pepper cheese on top of iceberg lettuce. Mama's is also a place for dessert with its traditional cannoli, an Italian pastry dessert meaning "little tube." The tube is stuffed with a sweet creamy filling containing ricotta, then served either plain or chocolate covered.

Antipasto Salad

Cannoli

Keith Hernandez and His Grill

Keith's Grill is named for Keith Hernandez, former MVP first baseman for the New York Mets. Keith won the Gold Glove award for eleven years in a row. Hernandez also guest starred in several classic episodes of the *Seinfeld* television show. The featured item at Keith's Grill is the Gold Glove Burger, a six-ounce hamburger patty on a toasted sesame bun with cheddar cheese, lettuce, tomato, dill pickle, raw onion, mayonnaise, with ketchup on the top bun and mustard on the bottom bun. Also offered is the Mets Burger, "created by Keith and his culinary team," with cheddar and Jack cheese, bacon, guacamole, chipotle aioli and jalapeños.

NEW YORK YANKEES

The new **Yankee Stadium** opened in 2009 next to the site of the iconic original Yankee Stadium built in 1923. The design of the new stadium follows the form of the old stadium. If Babe Ruth were around in 2009, he probably would have said "Some ball yard!" when he saw the new Yankee Stadium for the first time, as he said in 1923 when the original Yankee Stadium opened. Considering his prolific appetite, "The Babe" would approve of the food offerings at the new stadium.

Featured Hot Dog/Sausage

Nathan Handwerker started selling his hot dogs at Coney Island in 1916. They have been the best-known hot dogs in New York for nearly a century. Nathan's also sponsors the world-famous Fourth of July hot dog eating contest. Defending champion Joey Chestnut holds the record (set in 2013) for eating 69 Nathan's Famous hot dogs and buns in ten minutes. It is only fitting that Yankee Stadium has chosen Nathan's Famous as its hot dog provider. Varieties include the original, extra long, or natural casing hot dogs. The Bronx Bomber version (taking its name from the nickname of the Yankee team) includes chili, cheese, onion, sauerkraut, and relish. To enhance its hot dogs, Nathan's offers crinkle-cut fries and dipping sauces of chipotle aioli, bacon mayonnaise, or roasted garlic herb aioli.

Nathan's Hot Dog

More Hot Dogs and Sausages

For those who prefer an all-beef hot dog, Hebrew National has a stand at Yankee Stadium, where the hot dogs are topped with sauerkraut.

From the vast array of sausages manufactured by Premio Foods (a decades-old family business), two varieties are available at Yankee Stadium: Sweet/Mild Italian Sausage and Hot Italian Sausage. Both are served with onions and peppers.

Lobel's of New York

The Lobel family developed a meat business in Austria in the 1840s. When a grandson of the founder came to the U.S. in 1911, he brought the family butcher shop business to New York City, where it is now owned and operated by the fourth and fifth generations of the Lobel family. At Yankee Stadium, the Lobel stand offers exactly one item: a USDA prime beef steak sandwich. Judging by the long line, the one item offered is worth the wait.

Parm

Parm's restaurant (Mulberry Street in Manhattan) brings its classic meatball Parmesan sandwich to Yankee Stadium. Additionally, Parm's has a fresh mozzarella sandwich made with eggplant, cheese, tomato, fresh basil, and house spicy dressing. Both sandwiches are served hot.

Fresh Mozzarella Sandwich with Eggplant

Bazzini Nuts

Anthony Bazzini came to America from Italy in the 1800s. His first job was in a nut factory. After years of hard work, he bought the factory which has now operated under his name for more than 100 years. Bazzini peanuts and pistachios are sold throughout the stadium.

Masahiro Tanaka and the Tanaka Roll

The ONE Sushi serves a variety of rolls including California, veggie, spicy tuna, salmon, and shrimp tempura. Their signature roll is the Tanaka Roll, named for New York Yankees pitcher Masahiro Tanaka. Before coming to the Yankees in 2014, Tanaka pitched in Japan for the Tohoku Rakuten Golden Eagles and had a 24-0 record in 2013. The Tanaka Roll has shrimp tempura topped with spicy tuna, lobster meat salad, and wasabi mayonnaise.

Tanaka Roll

Chicken and Waffles

The first stand encountered when entering through the main gate at Yankee Stadium is Chicken and Waffles. Fried chicken patties are served between two waffles with maple syrup as a condiment. They come as an order of three sliders. The same stand offers a vanilla ice cream sandwich with waffles taking the place of traditional cookies.

Brother Jimmy's BBQ

With a slogan of "Put Some South in Yo' Mouth," Brother Jimmy's BBQ brings legendary North Carolina slow-smoking barbeque to Yankee Stadium. Fans can choose either a Carolina pulled-pork sandwich or a pulled barbeque chicken sandwich.

Malibu Roof Top Deck

The Malibu Roof Top Deck can be found on the top level at Yankee Stadium. This area is a popular hangout before the game for fans who want island-inspired grilled chicken jerk wings served with corn on the cob, or coconut-rum-glazed barbeque smoked ribs with cilantro and slaw. Also available is a bacon cheddar stuffed burger on a potato roll.

Pretzel Twist

Pretzel Twist

New York soft pretzels are sold throughout Yankee Stadium. In addition to the usual pretzel shape, they are available as a pretzel twist which resembles a loaf of bread.

Strictly Kosher

Strictly Kosher Inc. provides kosher food at Yankee Stadium. The stand offers a glatt kosher hot dog. For meat to be kosher, it must come from a kosher animal and be slaughtered in a kosher way. For meat to be glatt kosher, it must also come from an animal with adhesion-free or smooth lungs. Kosher laws require certification by a rabbi. This stand posts a certificate from Rabbi Vaad Harabonim of Queens. In addition to the hot dog, Strictly Kosher Inc. serves chicken nuggets, roast beef and chicken deli wraps, and potato knishes.

OAKLAND ATHLETICS

O.co Coliseum opened in 1966 as the home of the Oakland Raiders football team. It became home to the Athletics in 1968 when the team moved to Oakland from Kansas City. Today it is the only stadium that is home to both a Major League Baseball team and a National Football League team.

Featured Hot Dog/Sausage

The Oakland Athletics Atomic Hot Sausage has the reputation of being the hottest American-style sausage. It's the fresh onions and extra hot spices added to the beef and pork sausage that give it this reputation. Hickory smoked in a natural pork casing, the sausage is grilled and then topped with peppers and onions. The Atomic Hot Sausage is sold by Saag's. Saag's has produced authentic German sausages using old-world recipes since 1933 when George Saag opened a small butcher shop in downtown Oakland.

Atomic Hot Sausage

More Hot Dogs and Sausages

Saag's other ballpark sausages are the Sweet Italian, the Polish Sausage, the Hot Link, and the Bratwurst.

Also available at the New Belgium Brewing Company stand are three specialty hot dogs. The All Star Dog has macaroni and nacho cheese with jalapeños. The Diablo Dog has nacho cheese, bacon, and fried onion strings. The Bay Bridge Dog has chili and cheese.

There are several A's Grill carts, located throughout the stadium, serving jumbo dogs and Italian and Polish sausages with grilled onions and peppers.

Queen Margherita and Her Pizza

For pizza lovers, the White Elephant Brick Oven offers a margherita pizza with buffalo mozzarella cheese. A margherita pizza, with its red tomatoes, green basil, and white mozzarella, replicates the colors of the Italian flag. A popular legend holds that the margherita pizza was created to honor Queen Margherita when she was visiting the Royal Palace of Capodimonte in Naples in 1889. However, according to the BBC Food website, Zachary

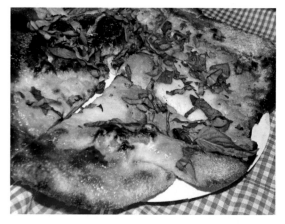

Margherita Pizza

Nowak, Assistant Director of Food Studies at the Umbra Institute in Perugia, Italy, raises doubts on the authenticity of the legend.

Seared Salmon Cake

Sold from a cart and prepared to order (takes about ten minutes) is the Seared Salmon Cake with frizzled onions and lemon dill aioli on a salt-and-pepper bun. A salt-and-pepper bun contains both sea salt and cracked pepper.

Cheeseburger Poppers

Ball Park Poppers

Ball Park Poppers are bite-size balls of deep-fried dough. They come in three varieties: jalapeño, cheeseburger, and corn dog. The poppers are topped with parsley and Parmesan cheese. Ball Park Poppers also sells full-size corn dogs. At most ballparks, corn dogs are prepared off site and frozen, then reheated at the park. At O.co Coliseum the hot dogs are dipped in batter and fried on site, as the customer watches.

Sweet Potato Pie

Sweet potato pie is a traditional side dish in the Southern United States, a soul food staple that probably came out of the African traditions of black slaves. It is often served during the American holiday season, especially at Thanksgiving. O.co's Ribs & Things stand serves it with whipped cream.

Gourmet Popcorn

Gourmet popcorn is available in seven flavors: caramel corn, cheddar cheese, spicy cheese, white cheddar, chocolate drizzle, birthday cake, and apple cinnamon. The popcorn cart also offers what it refers to as "Chicago style" popcorn, which is a mixture of cheddar cheese and caramel.

Sweet Potato Pie

PHILADELPHIA PHILLIES

Citizens Bank Park opened in 2004 and is part of the Philadelphia Sports Complex. The homes of the other three major Philadelphia sports teams are located within the Complex. The Philadelphia Eagles of the National Football League play at Lincoln Financial Field; the 76ers of the National Basketball Association and the Flyers of the National Hockey League play at the Wells Fargo Center.

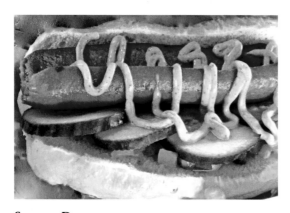

Summer Dog

Featured Hot Dog/Sausage

The Summer Dog comes with cucumber slices, peppers, onion, relish, and ancho chili sauce (a type of mole sauce made with mildly spicy ancho chilies.) It is available at The Philly Frank and Stein concessions stand. With the play on "Frankenstein" in the name of the stand, it's clear that not only hot dogs but beer is available here.

More Hot Dogs and Sausages

The Old Bay Signature Sausage is a sweet Italian sausage covered with grilled peppers and onions and topped with Old Bay Seasoning. This blend of 18 herbs and spices is a standard in the Chesapeake Bay region, found on most restaurant and home tables along with salt and pepper. Old Bay's name was inspired by a steamship line that once traveled between Maryland and Virginia.

As one would expect in Philadelphia, there is a Cheesesteak Dog at the ballpark. The hot dog is topped with chopped steak, onions, and melted cheese.

The Schmitter

There is a common misbelief that The Schmitter is named for Mike Schmidt, Hall-of-Famer third baseman who played for the Phillies from 1973 to 1989. In reality, it was invented in the 1920s at

The Schmitter

McNally's Quick Lunch in the Chestnut Hill area of Philadelphia. The Schmitter was named after Schmidt's beer. It is described as "Philadelphia's Big League Sandwich." Sliced beef is topped with cheese, fried onions, tomatoes, grilled salami, and Schmitter sauce and then served on a flash-broiled Conshohocken kaiser roll. The Schmitter sauce, which has the look of Thousand Island dressing, is a "secret" recipe. The Conshohocken Italian bakery opened in the Philadelphia suburb of Conshohocken in 1973.

Philadelphia Cheesesteak

The food that people most associate with Philadelphia is the cheesesteak. Two of Philadelphia's best known cheesesteak providers have stands at Citizens Bank Park.

Tony Luke's describes its cheesesteaks as "the real taste of South Philly." It uses thinly sliced Black Angus beef carefully chosen from humanely raised cattle. Customers can add the cheese of their choice (American, Cheez Whiz, or provolone). Another choice at Tony Luke's is its roast pork sandwich. Garlicky pork, sliced thin, is served au jus on a roll.

Campo's advertises itself as "the best place for authentic Philadelphia food." Its cheesesteak sandwich choices are The Heater or The Works. The Heater is a spicy cheesesteak made with jalapeño cheddar cheese and buffalo hot sauce. The Works adds sweet bell peppers, mushrooms, fried onions and provolone cheese. The cheesesteaks can be accompanied by local favorite Herr's potato chips.

Chickie's and Pete's Crabfries

The most crowded stand on the day we visited Citizens Bank Park was Chickie's and Pete's Crabfries. When Chickie's and Pete's opened in Philadelphia in 1977 as a crab house and sports bar, it sold crab mainly in the summer. Pete wanted a way to use the leftover crab seasoning during the winter, so he experimented with putting it on French fries. After two winters of trying different combinations and asking his customers for their opinions, Pete settled on what has become his signature crinkle-cut Crabfries.

Crabfries

Federal Donuts

Federal Donuts is a Philadelphia institution that serves fried chicken with donuts. Every order of chicken includes Japanese cucumber pickles and a honey donut. The chicken can be original style or cooked with either buttermilk-ranch seasoning or a chili-garlic glaze. For those who want their donuts chicken-less, vanilla spice and cinnamon brown sugar varieties are available.

Pennsylvania Dutch Funnel Cake

The Pennsylvania Dutch Funnel Cake stand serves its deep-fried cakes topped with powdered sugar and either strawberries or apples. The funnel cake mix comes from the Funnel Cake Factory which traces its origin back to Lorraine Wilson. Mrs. Wilson

Funnel Cake with Strawberries

was a supper-club singer who founded a family-run funnel cake business in 1974. Using her grandmother's recipe, she began selling at local fairs in Pennsylvania.

Water Ice

The Philadelphia Water Ice Factory stand sells three flavors of water ice (sometimes known as Italian ice). Water ice is a frozen dessert similar to ice cream but made without dairy products or eggs. Flavorings come from fruit concentrates, juices or purees. Flavors available at Citizens Bank Park are cherry, lemon, and mango.

BBQ Chicken Platter

Greg "The Bull" Luzinski's BBQ

Left fielder Greg "The Bull" Luzinski, an All-Star player with the Phillies, opened Bull's BBQ at Citizens Bank Park. He tries to attend every home game to meet with fans and share his love of barbeque. The Bull offers pulled pork sandwiches, pit beef sandwiches, ribs, turkey legs, hot dogs, and half-roast-chicken plates. Baked beans and cole slaw are served as side dishes. All the meats are cooked with The Bull BBQ Sauce, which is also sold by the bottle at the stand and in many area grocery stores.

Hoagies

In addition to cheesesteak, Philadelphia is known for hoagies. Called by different names throughout the country, a hoagie is a sandwich built on a long bread roll and filled with a variety of meats, cheeses, vegetables and seasonings. Citizens Bank Park serves several varieties of hoagies: turkey, ham and cheese, roast beef, or vegetarian.

PITTSBURGH PIRATES

PNC Park opened in 2001. It is located along the Allegheny River on the North Shore of Pittsburgh, with a panoramic view of the Pittsburgh skyline. The architects modeled the stadium after historic Forbes Field, home of the Pittsburgh Pirates from 1909 to 1970.

Featured Hot Dog/Sausage

Polish Hill is a residential neighborhood in Pittsburgh which is also home to the Immaculate Heart of Mary church, the oldest and largest in Pittsburgh. The neighborhood was settled in the nineteenth century by Polish immigrants who came to work in the steel industry. The Polish Hill Dog is topped with mini potato pierogies and homemade onion straws, with cole slaw spread on the bun.

Polish Hill Dog

More Hot Dogs and Sausages

The Federal Street Grill offers a Polish kielbasa and an Italian sausage, both topped with grilled peppers and onions. Sausages at PNC Park are provided by Silver Star Meats of nearby McKees Rocks. Silver Star Meats, founded in 1964, provides products from Eastern European traditions dating back to the late 1800s.

Buns for hot dogs at PNC Park are made by Cellone's Italian Bread Company of Pittsburgh. The Cellone family came to Pittsburgh in 1911 from Torino, Italy. They started baking breads in their home and delivering them door-to-door throughout the neighborhood, using a horse-drawn wagon. Cellone's is said to be the first bakery in the United States to produce the egg bun, which has become an American bakery standard.

Primanti Brothers

In the early 1930s, Joe Primanti set up a cart in Pittsburgh, selling sandwiches to hungry truckers who were coming and going at all times of the night. Encouraged by his success, he opened a storefront on 18th Street, along with his brothers Dick and Stanley and their nephew John DePriter. They became the Primanti Brothers, operating a chain of restaurants throughout the Pittsburgh area. Primanti Brothers is best known for serving sandwiches with French-fried potatoes and cole slaw incorporated into the sandwich filling. At

Primanti Brothers Roast Beef Sandwich

PNC Park, two of its specialty sandwiches are offered, both topped with French fries, cole slaw and tomatoes on white French bread. The choice is either roast beef and cheese or capicola and cheese. Capicola is a traditional Italian cold cut made from the dry-cured muscle running from the neck to the fourth or fifth rib of a pork shoulder. (It probably tastes better than it sounds.) Primanti Brothers also offers a traditional cheesesteak sandwich.

Chicken Gyros

Papa Dukes Gyros

George and Dorothea Papas, along with their adult children Perry and Frances, opened their first restaurant in 1982. It was known as Papa Duke's Paris Grill. A second location, Papa Duke's Bar and Grill, opened in 2008. At PNC Park Papa Duke's has a gyros stand. Gyros is a Greek dish with meat roasted on a vertical spit. The meat, thinly sliced off the spit, is served in a pita bread pocket with tomato, onion, lettuce and tzatziki sauce. Tzatziki is made from strained yogurt mixed with cucumbers, garlic, salt, olive oil and lemon juice. Papa Duke's gyros come with a choice of beef or chicken.

Pierogi

A pierogi (with many different spellings) is a filled dumpling of unleavened dough, first broiled and then baked or fried. Pierogies are traditionally stuffed with cheese, potato filling, ground meat, or fruit. They are usually semicircular in shape, but can be made in other shapes. They are of Eastern European origin. At PNC Park, fans can order Mrs. T's cheese pierogies, a four-cheese medley of aged cheddar, Parmesan, romano, and Swiss cheese. Mrs. T (Mary Twardzik) and her son Ted started making pierogies in 1952 in Shenandoah, Pennsylvania. Today Mrs. T's sells over one-half billion pierogies a year in grocery stores and at restaurants throughout the country.

Seaweed Salad

Seaweed Salad

Nakama Japanese Steakhouse and Sushi Bar has been voted the best sushi in Pittsburgh for eight consecutive years by *Pittsburgh Magazine*. At PNC Park, Nakama Express offers sushi, hibachi meats, udon noodles, egg rolls, fried rice, and seaweed salad. (I believe Harry M. Stevens never hawked seaweed salad himself.) Seaweed is a good source of fiber and has many other nutritional values including being one of the best sources of iodine. The seaweed salad at Nakama Express is made with sesame seeds and a vinaigrette dressing.

Pirates Buried Treasure

Cold Cow Ice Cream is a family-owned business based in Pittsburgh, specializing in using locally-sourced ingredients. One special flavor offered at PNC Park is Pirates Buried Treasure, fudge ripple ice cream blended with peanut butter cups.

Rita's Italian Ice

In 1984 Pennsylvania former firefighter Bob Tumolo started selling Italian ice from a small porch window in Bensalem, Pennsylvania, with the goal of earning a little extra income. He named the business after his wife, Rita. He more than achieved his goal, and Rita's Italian Ice now has over 500 locations. At PNC Park this dairy-free frozen dessert comes in flavors such as mango, mint chocolate chip, cookies and cream, strawberry colada, and Swedish Fish (soft chewy fish-shaped candies).

Willie Stargell and Pops Plaza

Willie Stargell, nicknamed Pops, played his entire 21-year major league career in Pittsburgh as an outfielder and first baseman. He led his team to World Series championships in 1971 and 1979 and was inducted into the Baseball Hall of Fame in 1988. Four concessions stands are part of Pops Plaza, honoring Willie Stargell. Joining Nakama Express and Chickie's and Pete's at Pops Plaza are Chicken on the Hill and the Familee BBQ.

Tatchos

In addition to chicken tenders and French fries, Chicken on the Hill offers its unique creation, Tatchos. Tatchos are tater tots covered with sour cream, chili, cheese, and jalapeños.

Familee BBQ

"We Are Family," a song by Sister Sledge, was the theme song for the 1979 World Series champion Pittsburgh Pirates. This might be the inspiration for the Familee BBQ stand at Pops Plaza. The stand serves all-beef jumbo hot dogs, one-half-pound burgers, pulled pork nachos, and a pulled pork pierogi stacker (a pulled pork sandwich with pierogies on top.)

Manny Sanguillen

Manny Sanguillen played for the Pittsburgh Pirates as a catcher during 13 of his 14 years in the major leagues. His .296 lifetime batting average is tenth highest for catchers in major league history. Legendary Pittsburgh Pirate Roberto Clemente was killed in 1972 in an airline disaster while taking relief supplies to victims of an earthquake in Nicaragua. Clemente had invited his best friend, Manny Sanguillen, to join him on the flight. When Sanguillen was ready to go to the airport he could not find his car keys, thus missing the flight and saving his life.

Manny's BBQ stand at PNC Park is known for its grilled Angus burger, a chargrilled one-half-pound Angus burger topped with American cheese and Manny's signature barbeque sauce. Angus beef comes originally from Angus County in Scotland. Black Angus is now the most common breed

Shrooms Burger

of beef cattle in the United States. Manny's BBQ also sells a pulled pork sandwich.

BR-GR (Burger)

The BR-GR stand says, "Our beef is a handcrafted blend of sirloin, chuck, rib eye, and strip ground fresh daily." It offers four specialty hamburgers. The Abso-Bac'n-Lutely Burger adds bacon to three cheeses (American, provolone, pepper jack). The Shrooms Burger has forest mushrooms, caramelized onions, provolone, and whole grain mustard aioli. The Fire in the Hole Burger has guacamole, jalapeños, pepper jack cheese, chipotle aioli, and sriracha sauce. The California Lovin' Burger is actually a turkey burger. It is topped with provolone, oven-roasted tomatoes, pesto mayo, alfalfa sprouts, and guacamole.

Quaker Steak and Lube

At the Quaker Steak and Lube stand boneless wings and onion rings are offered. (I am not sure why you would name a food stand as a takeoff on motor oil. I am further puzzled by the fact that the stand sells chicken rather than steak.) The sauces for the wings are Arizona Ranch, Louisiana Lickers, BBQ Hot and BBQ Medium. Its onion rings are known as O-Rings, a pun on o-rings, a common automobile component.

Healthy Options

The Just4U stand offers "healthy options." Several salads are available including the tomato and mozzarella salad with oven-dried grape tomatoes tossed in olive oil and basil, served with fresh mozzarella and balsamic dressing. The Caprese Toaster is a sandwich with sliced tomatoes and mozzarella served on gluten-free bread with fresh basil and a balsamic glaze.

CULINARY TOUR OF THE MAJOR LEAGUE BALLPARKS

SAN DIEGO PADRES

Petco Park opened in 2004 in downtown San Diego, part of the trend of building ballparks in the middle of urban centers. There was no need for a retractable roof as the Padres average one rainout for every seven years.

Featured Hot Dog/Sausage

Randy Jones, a former Padres pitcher and Cy Young Award winner, moved from baseball to a career in catering and restaurants. He opened the All-American Sports Grill in downtown San Diego. The Randy Jones Grill at Petco Park features hot dogs, sausages, and sliders. The "K" Basa is a one-half pound kielbasa sausage. "K" is the symbol for strikeout on a baseball scorecard.

"K" Basa

More Hot Dogs and Sausages

Also available at the Randy Jones Grill are The Slugger Dog, a one-half pound hot dog, and the Hi Heat Link, a one-third pound hot link sausage.

Friar Franks

The traditional hot dogs at Petco Park are called Friar Franks and are provided by the hot dog chain Wienerschnitzel. Wienerschnitzel (sometimes known as Der Wienerschnitzel) has hundreds of locations throughout California and the Southwest. The Wienerschnitzel website has a timeline of the history of the hot dog. Interestingly, it incorrectly credits Harry M. Stevens and cartoonist Tad Dorgan with coining the phrase "hot dog." (See "The Hot Dog Comes to Baseball" chapter.)

El Toro Tri-Tip Sandwich

In 2013, *USA Today* asked fans of all 30 major league teams to vote on their favorite ballpark food in the Stadium Food King Challenge. The winner was the El Toro Tri-Tip Sandwich at Petco Park. The sandwich is provided by Phil's BBQ, a local San Diego favorite. Phil's BBQ stand also serves baby back ribs and pulled pork sandwiches.

El Toro Tri-Tip Sandwich

THE JOY OF BALLPARK FOOD: FROM HOT DOGS TO HAUTE CUISINE

Seafood Burritos

For the many fans of Mexican cuisine in the San Diego area, Petco Park has a variety of options. Both Lucha Libre and Miguel's Cocina sell versions of meat and seafood burritos. The Lucha Libre's Surfin' California Burrito was featured on the Travel Channel television show *Man v. Food*. This burrito is stuffed with grilled steak, shrimp, French fries, avocado, pico de gallo, cheese, and super-secret chipotle sauce. Miquel's Cocina describes their Surf 'n Turf Burrito as "an epic 1 lb. burrito."

Hodad's

Local San Diego burger place Hodad's has a cart at Petco Field. The cart is decorated with license plates from many states. The menu is simple: hamburgers, cheeseburgers, and fries. *www.cnn.com* listed Hodad's as one of its "Five Tasty Burger Joints Worth Visiting."

Anthony's Fish Grotto

When World War II ended in 1945, Anthony and Tod Ghio and their friend Roy Weber returned home to help "Mama" Ghio open a seafood restaurant on the San Diego waterfront. Using old-world recipes from her days in Italy, "Mama" Ghio's menu has been served for over sixty years. At Petco Park, Anthony's Fish Grotto continues the tradition with fish and chips, shrimp and chips, shrimp avocado salad, and clam chowder.

Bumble Bee Tuna

Bumble Bee Seafoods moved its corporate headquarters in 2014 to an unoccupied historic building located adjacent to Petco Park. Bumble Bee is one of the leading sellers of canned tuna. The stand at Petco Park offers a grilled tuna melt, a tuna Nicoise salad (a French salad popular in the seaside town of Nice), and a tuna salad sandwich with vine-ripened tomatoes, golden raisins, and arugula served on a ciabatta roll.

Southpaw Sliders

In addition to hot dogs and sausages, the Randy Jones Grill at Petco Park offers two varieties of Southpaw Sliders. Randy was a left-handed pitcher (referred to as a southpaw). The garlic marinated steak sliders are topped with blue cheese spread. The chipotle chicken sliders have chimichuri spread (a green sauce of Argentinian origins using minced garlic, parsley, olive oil, oregano and wine vinegar). Both sliders come with sides of summer squash and kettle chips.

Seaside Market

The Seaside Market serves a burgundy pepper tri-tip sandwich on a brioche roll. It comes with a choice of two sides from a list of gooey mac 'n cheese, crispy potato wedges, pineapple cole slaw, or country applewood-smoked bacon potato salad. Also available are nachos topped with sliced tri-tip. The Seaside Market also serves unique salads including Spicy Tofu Noodle Salad with sweet peppers, cilantro, orzo, sun-dried tomatoes and feta cheese or California Kale and Avocado Salad with oregano vinaigrette.

California Kale and Avocado Salad

Rimel's Rotisserie

Rimel's Rotisserie provides fish tacos made with grilled chunks of fresh mahi-mahi and served with black beans and rice. As its name implies, rotisserie chicken is available fresh off the spit. In the California fusion food tradition, Rimel's also offers Chinese-style dishes such as pot stickers and "wok'd" bowls. The "wok'd" bowls include vegetables, rice, and the choice of chicken or mahi-mahi.

Mahi-Mahi Taco

Chocolat Bistro Creperie Cremerie

The Chocolat Bistro Creperie Cremerie serves sweet and savory homemade crepes. The sweet crepes may be chocolate or Nutella and come with a choice of bananas or strawberries. The savory crepes are ham and cheese or a four-cheese combination.

The Baked Bear

The Baked Bear sells custom ice cream cookie sandwiches. Each customer chooses a cookie for the top, a cookie for the bottom, and a flavor of ice cream. The varieties of cookies and ice cream flavors change daily. We chose a red velvet top cookie, a snickerdoodle bottom, and mint chip ice cream.

Ice Cream Cookie Sandwich

SAN FRANCISCO GIANTS

AT&T Park opened in 2000, located in the "South of Market" neighborhood of San Francisco, overlooking San Francisco Bay. McCovey Cove (named for former Giants first baseman Willie McCovey) is the unofficial name of the section of San Francisco Bay beyond the right field wall of AT&T Park. During games small boats anchor in the Cove hoping to retrieve home run balls known as "splash hits."

Featured Hot Dog/Sausage

Tres Agave (literally, three agave plants) is the San Francisco restaurant that supplies AT&T Park with the Tres Agave Dog. This hot dog would be at home on a street cart in Tijuana, Mexico. The wiener has a bacon wrap, spicy chipotle mayonnaise, sweet grilled onions, and cucumber pico de gallo.

Tres Agave Dog

More Hot Dogs and Sausages

The Chicago Dog stand (serving Hebrew National products) offers three regional hot dogs. The Chicago Dog is topped with mustard, relish, onion, tomato, pickle, sport peppers and celery salt. The Coney Island Dog comes with chili, cheddar cheese and onions. The San Francisco Dog has Swiss cheese, sauerkraut, onion, pickle spears, and Thousand Island sauce.

The Doggie Diner at AT&T Park is named after the iconic fast food restaurant chain that flourished in the San Francisco Bay Area from 1948 to 1986. The AT&T Doggie Diner features hot dogs from the Eisenberg Sausage Company, founded in 1929.

At the Say Hey! sausage stand (baseball great Willie Mays was known as "The Say Hey Kid"), fans have their choice of Italian sausage, bratwurst (regular or cooked with beer), Louisiana hot link, chicken apple sausage, pineapple sausage, Polish kielbasa, pepper jack hickory-smoked sausage, as well as an all-beef colossal dog.

McCovey's Restaurant serves a traditional stadium dog, a Polish dog, and a hot link.

Edsel Ford Fong

Edsel Ford Fong was a well-known waiter at the Sam Wo Restaurant in San Francisco's Chinatown. He was often called the world's rudest, worst, and most insulting waiter. Legendary *San Francisco Chronicle* columnist Herb Caen included Fong as

Edamame

#58 in his guide of things to do in San Francisco: "See the world's rudest waiter." The Edsel Ford Fong stand at AT&T Park serves standard Chinese fare including crispy orange chicken, beef with broccoli, and vegetable fried rice. It also serves edamame (young soybeans in the pod).

Ghirardelli Chocolate

One of the best-known San Francisco treats is Ghirardelli chocolate. The Ghirardelli Chocolate Company began in San Francisco in 1852 and per their website is "one of the few original and continuously operating businesses in California." Domingo Ghirardelli, its founder, was the son and apprentice of an Italian chocolatier. In 1849 he moved to San Francisco first to join the gold prospectors, and later to sell tired miners chocolate candies. Part of Ghirardelli's great success for so long is due to its complete control of the manufacturing process (from cocoa bean selection to finished product) and innovative use of advertising. At AT&T Park, fans can order either the classic hot fudge sundae or ice cream served in a waffle cone.

Ghiradelli Sundae

Orlando's Caribbean BBQ

Orlando's Caribbean BBQ is owned by former Giant slugger Orlando Cepeda. Its signature item is the Cha Cha Bowl which consists of jerk chicken, white rice, black beans, and pineapple salsa. It also serves a Cuban sandwich (pork loin, ham, Swiss cheese and pickles on a panini roll) as well as a wide variety of nachos. The sweet potato fries are topped with a cinnamon chipotle sprinkle.

North Beach

North Beach is an area of San Francisco known as "Little Italy" and the childhood home of Joe DiMaggio. North Beach – A Taste of San Francisco at AT&T Park offers three classics found in North Beach restaurants. The catchiest name goes to the Stinking Rose 40 Clove Garlic Chicken Sandwich. It also serves a meatball sandwich and a ravioli bowl.

Crazy Crab'z

The Crazy Crab'z serves a traditional San Francisco crab sandwich consisting of fresh Dungeness crab salad on grilled sourdough bread with tomatoes. Salad lovers can get a crab and shrimp salad or a Crab Louie salad.

Crab Sandwich

Murph's Irish Pub

Murph's Irish Pub serves a classic grilled Reuben sandwich (corned beef, Swiss cheese, and sauerkraut on rye). It also sells Irish Nachos -- French fries covered with chili, cheddar cheese, and jalapeños.

Pier 44 Chowder House

The Pier 44 Chowder House offers the famous San Francisco clam chowder in a sourdough bread bowl. Seafood lovers can also choose traditional fish and chips, shrimp and chips, or fried calamari.

Lamb

At most ballparks, lamb lovers would be out of luck. At AT&T Park, however, there is not one but two locations serving lamb. The Anchor Grill and the California Cookout each serves its own variety of lamb sausage.

'Outta Here Cheesesteak

'Outta Here Cheesesteak is named for the familiar baseball announcer's call for a home run. In addition to the original Philly Cheesesteak, it serves a San Francisco variety with grilled chicken, mushrooms, onions, Cheez Whiz, and the choice of sweet or hot peppers. The veggie cheesesteak features Cheez Whiz, shredded zucchini, grilled tomatoes, mushrooms, onions and peppers. All of the cheesesteaks are served on traditional Amoroso rolls. Amoroso's Baking Company is a five-generation family-owned Philadelphia company producing hearth-baked rolls and bread.

Fresh Roasted Peanuts

The fresh roasted peanut stand has its own peanut roasting machine where you can watch the peanuts whirling around as they roast. The roasting machine was manufactured by C. Cretors & Co. of Chicago, which entered the concessions machine business in 1885.

Biscotti and Madeleines

For those who want an out-of-the-ordinary sweet treat, the @Café, an internet café within the ballpark, serves biscotti and madeleines.

SEATTLE MARINERS

Safeco Field is a retractable-roof stadium located in the SoDo district of Seattle. SoDo is the "South of Downtown" area of Seattle, near the historic Pioneer Square. Next door is the site of CenturyLink Field, home of the Seattle Seahawks football team.

Featured Hot Dog/Sausage

Ethan Stowell is a celebrated chef and owner of restaurants in the Seattle area. Stowell was named by *Food & Wine Magazine* as one of the "Best New Chefs in America" in 2008. Since 2010 Ethan has been working with the Seattle Mariners on the food offerings at Safeco Field. Ethan Stowell's Hamburg + Frites, as the name implies, sells hamburgers and French fries. It also offers, however, a signature hot dog known as the Pen Seattle Dog. The stand is located in The Pen, an area in centerfield behind the Mariners' bullpen. The Pen Seattle Dog comes with cream cheese, banana peppers, and onions. I've often seen cream cheese on bagels and occasionally turkey sandwiches, but this is the first time I've seen it on a hot dog.

Pen Seattle Dog

More Hot Dogs and Sausages

The traditional hot dog at Safeco Field comes in three sizes with names as confusing as Starbucks' *tall, grande,* and *venti.* (Starbucks was founded in Seattle.) The "tall" hot dog is called the SoDo Dog. The "grande" version is called the Mariners Dog. The "venti" is called the Foot-long Dog.

At the Safeco Field Sausage Company stand are cheddar bratwurst, sweet Italian sausages, and Polish sausages. They are all served with grilled onions, banana peppers, and Riesling sauerkraut. According to the Total Wine & More website, "Washington State produces high-quality Riesling."

Veggie Dogs and Burgers

The Natural stand sells veggie burgers and veggie dogs. The veggie dog is made by local Seattle company Field Roast. Seattle chef David Lee learned of the Asian tradition of using grains as the foundations of vegetarian "meat." By adding European flavors, he developed a new version of grain meat used at Field Roast.

Swingin' Wings

Swingin' Wings is another stand created by Chef Ethan Stowell. Chicken wings are available in classic, honey serrano, or barbeque varieties. For those who like fried foods other than potatoes, fried cheese curds and fried pickles are interesting alternatives.

Ivar's

Ivar's is a Seattle seafood icon. Ivar Haglund, known in Seattle in the 1930s as a folksinger, opened the first Seattle aquarium on the Puget Sound waterfront in 1938, exhibiting sea life that he had collected from the Sound. Seeing that aquarium visitors were hungry, he soon added Ivar's Fish Bar where he sold clam chowder and fish and chips. Today Ivar's has expanded to include full-service restaurants and fish bars in many locations.

At Safeco Field, in addition to clam chowder, salads, and fish and chips, Ivar's offers two signature sandwiches. Advertised as "Seattle's Fish Sandwich," the Ivar Dog is fried and freshly breaded Pacific cod, cole slaw and tartar sauce on a roll. The other specialty is the Grilled Wild Alaska Salmon Sandwich. Ivar's uses salmon from the Yukon River.

Edgar's Cantina

Growing up in Mexico City, Roberto Santibañez learned to make tamales and salsa from his grandmother. Migrating to the U.S. in 1997, he brought his restaurant ideas first to Texas, then New York City. His stand at Safeco field, Edgar's Cantina, makes torta sandwiches. A Mexcian torta sandwich is served on an oblong crusty sandwich roll. Edgar's tortas are toasted and filled with either carne asada, pork carnitas, chicken Milanese or salchicha (sausage). The stand is named for former Seattle Mariner great Edgar Martinez.

Chicken Caesar Pizzetti

Chicken Caesar Pizzetti

Modern Apizza has long been a local tradition in New Haven, Connecticut. Now, 2,932 miles from New Haven, owner and chef Bill Pustari has opened a concession stand at Safeco Field called Apizza. Pizza varieties are cheese, pepperoni, and wild mushroom. Appiza also serves pizzetti, a single-serving Neapolitan-style thin crust pizza, topped with Caesar salad or chicken Caesar salad.

Thai Ginger

Local Seattle restaurant Thai Ginger has opened the Thai Ginger International Wok at Safeco Field. Offerings include garlic beef, chicken curry, cashew chicken, and pad Thai vegetables.

ShiskaBerry's

ShiskaBerry's has been selling chocolate-dipped fruit on a stick at sporting events and concerts since 1998 in the western United States. At Safeco Field fans can get the Double Play, fresh strawberries dipped in white and milk chocolate. The Berry I'bananez is a skewer of banana chunks and strawberries dipped in a choice of white, milk or dark chocolate. This treat is named after former Seattle Mariner Raúl Ibañez.

Vegan Steamed Buns

Vegan Steamed Buns

Bao Choi serves vegan steamed buns. The buns are similar to the style often served with Peking duck. Two choices of fillings are offered. The first contains black vinegar-glazed portobello mushrooms, green chili and cucumber salad, basil, and siracha mayonnaise. The second has gochujang-glazed eggplant, cilantro cabbage slaw, and kimchee mayonnaise. (Gochujang is a savory fermented Korean condiment made from red chili, rice and soybeans.)

Banana Peppers

Uncle Charlie's Cheesesteak serves the usual cheesesteak except for the type of pepper. Mild, tangy banana peppers are used instead of the usual bell peppers. I counted four different stands at Safeco Field that use banana peppers but cannot find a Seattle banana pepper connection.

Fried Twinkie

Fried Twinkie

Fair Territory sells favorites traditionally sold at county and state fairs. Ballpark fans can choose from funnel cake, churros, corn dogs, or the infamous fried Twinkies. Fortunately for those who think a Twinkie is too healthy for you, one can now add the deep-fried element.

ST. LOUIS CARDINALS

Busch Stadium opened in 2006 in downtown St. Louis. Outside the stadium is St. Louis Ballpark Village, a newly developed area containing retail shops, restaurants, and residential units. The highest attendance for a sporting event at Busch Stadium was not a baseball game, but rather a soccer match between Chelsea Football Club and Manchester City Football Club played in 2013.

Bacon-Wrapped Dog

Meat Knish

Featured Hot Dog/Sausage

Hunter Hot Dogs are "the official hot dog of the St. Louis Cardinals." The Hunter bacon-wrapped dog is a jumbo dog topped with baked beans, French-fried onion strings, sauerkraut, pico de gallo, and barbeque sauce.

More Hot Dogs and Sausages

For fans who prefer beef hot dogs, several carts throughout the stadium sell Nathan's All-Beef Jumbo Dogs. For fans who want the hot dog experience without red meat, chicken bratwurst is available.

Pretzels and bratwurst are popular ballpark foods. The Triple Play stand decided to go for a double play with the Bratzel, a bratwurst wrapped inside a pretzel.

Kohn's Kosher Knishes and Knockwurst

Kohn's offers kosher food at Busch Stadium. Kohn's is a kosher restaurant founded in St. Louis by Simon and Bobbie Kohn in 1963. At Busch Stadium pastrami and corned beef sandwiches are served with potato salad. Kosher hot dogs and knockwurst, along with meat and potato knishes, are also sold. The knishes are made locally and are baked instead of fried.

MoonPies and Cherry Licorice

The Plaza Grill offers two regional sweets. MoonPies have been made at the Chattanooga Bakery since 1917. MoonPies consist of two round graham cracker cookies with marshmallow filling between them, then dipped in chocolate. Cherry licorice at the Plaza Grill comes from the Switzer Candy Company. Frederick Switzer was born in St. Louis in 1865. His father died when Frederick was young, and the boy needed to raise money to help support his family. He would walk the riverfront area of St. Louis, peddling candies from a cart. Eventually he started the Switzer Candy Company, which remains a St. Louis business to this day.

Smoked Beef Brisket Sandwich

Smoked beef brisket with Cardinal Nation Chips (homemade kettle-cooked barbequed potato chips) is sold from a cart where the brisket is hand-sliced as you wait. Cardinal Nation refers to the fans of the St. Louis Cardinals throughout portions of the Midwest and South. "Our house-smoked beef brisket is served on a fresh Kaiser roll with red onions, dill pickles, and bourbon BBQ sauce."

Smoked Brisket Sandwich

Island Grill

The Island Grill offers three unique specialties. Mahi-Mahi Tacos come with lettuce, pico de gallo and chipotle mayo. Crab Cake Sliders are served with pickles and roasted red pepper remoulade. The Spicy Shrimp Hoagie sandwich comes with lettuce, pico de gallo and lemon-caper aioli.

Dizzy's Diner

Dizzy's Diner is named for former St. Louis ballplayer Dizzy Dean. Dizzy Dean was the last National League pitcher to win 30 games in one season, and was elected to the Baseball Hall of Fame in 1953. Available at Dizzy's Diner are hot dogs, bratwurst, corn dogs, Polish sausage, hamburgers, cheeseburgers, chicken sandwiches and chicken tenders.

Spicy Shrimp Hoagie

Asian Stir Fry

Made-to-order Chinese food is available at the Asian Stir Fry stand. Fans choose either fried rice or noodles and either chicken, beef or shrimp. The selection is freshly cooked on site in a wok with green and red peppers, cabbage, mushrooms, onions, peapods and carrots.

Double Play Tap and Grill

At the Double Play Tap and Grill the nachos are so large that they are called Four Hands Nacho Platter (maybe because you need four hands to carry the plate). The chips are topped with Monterey Jack and shredded queso fresco cheeses, pico de gallo, scallions, jalapeños, sour cream, and a choice of beef, chicken, or pork. The Double Play also serves flatbread pizzas. The barbequed pork pizza has red onions, banana peppers, Gouda and mozzarella cheeses. The carnita chicken pizza has olives, salsa, jalapeños, Jack and cheddar cheeses. The spinach artichoke pizza comes with Alfredo sauce, Parmesan and mozzarella cheeses.

Spinach Artichoke Flatbread Pizza

Free Ice Cream

There may be no such thing as a free lunch but on Sundays at Busch Stadium there is free vanilla ice cream. Prairie Farms offers all fans an ice cream cup as part of their ice cream "Sunday" promotion.

TAMPA BAY RAYS

Tropicana Field is the only domed stadium in the major leagues. It has been the host of the Tampa Bay Rays since the expansion team's inaugural season in 1998. The stadium is located in St. Petersburg, one of the major cities of the Tampa Bay area.

Featured Hot Dog/Sausage

As is the case at Marlins Park, hot dogs and sausages play a minor role in the food offerings at Tropicana Field. In addition to the traditional hot dog and sausage, fans can get an Italian Sausage with onions and peppers served on pizza bread instead of a traditional bun.

Italian Sausage on Pizza Bread

More Hot Dogs and Sausages

Hot dogs are provided by Kayem Foods, makers of the famous Fenway Frank. The Kayem hot dog topped with chili and cheese is known as The Heater. The Slaw Dog is topped with cole slaw, nacho cheese, salsa, and jalapeños, and served on a poppyseed bun.

Bloomin' Onion

Outback Steakhouse, the Australian-themed steakhouse restaurant, has a stand at Tropicana Field. It serves a steak sandwich with mushrooms and grilled chicken on the barbie. The grilled chicken is prepared in strips and served with a barbeque sauce. Also available is Outback's signature item, the Bloomin' Onion. According to its website, "Our special onion is hand-carved by a dedicated bloomologist, cooked until golden and ready to dip into our spicy signature bloom sauce." When served, the Bloomin' Onion looks like a flower with its petals spread.

Bloomin' Onion

Beignets

Carni Classics sells hot beignets (squares of fried dough sprinkled with powdered sugar.) The most famous beignets are sold at the Café du Monde in New Orleans. The original Café du Monde coffee stand opened in 1862 in the New Orleans French Market.

Everglades BBQ Company

The Everglades BBQ Company offers pulled smoked pork sandwiches and pulled smoked pork nachos. The server at the stand literally pulls the pork by hand to make each sandwich. Provided at the nearby condiment stand are eight varieties of Everglades BBQ sauces.

Cuban Burger

Tropicana Field offers several Cuban-style items. At the Burger Up! stand, the Cuban Burger consists of two all-beef patties topped with ham, Genoa salami, Cuban pork, Swiss cheese, pickle planks, and a secret mustard sauce. The Grand Slam Grill serves Cuban sandwiches (layers of ham, pork, cheese, pickles and mustard on a grilled roll.)

Cuban Burger

Gourmet Grilled Cheese Sandwich

The Gourmet Grilled Cheese Sandwich stand serves roast beef sandwiches. (Just kidding, but I'm not sure what makes these grilled cheese sandwiches "gourmet.") This stand serves grilled cheese sandwiches either plain, with bacon, or with tomato.

Italian Beef

The Italian Beef Sandwich stand offers "slow oven-roasted, perfectly Italian seasoned beef, sliced thin and served with mild giardiniera." Giardiniera, which means "under vinegar," is an Italian-American relish of pickled vegetables in vinegar or oil.

Turkey on Marble Rye

The Carvery serves hand-carved roasted turkey sandwiches on marble rye bread. Contrary to popular belief, the dark swirl in marble rye is not pumpernickel but is made darker with the addition of cocoa powder. (This is a fun fact that you can share at your next office party.)

Boiled Peanuts

In addition to the ordinary roasted peanuts, Tropicana Field offers boiled peanuts, a Southern specialty. After boiling in salt water, the peanuts (still in their shells) take on a strong salty taste and become soft, somewhat resembling a cooked pea

Boiled Peanuts

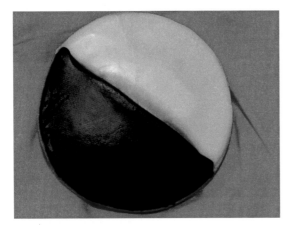

Black and White Cookie

or a bean. Since the eighteenth century, boiling peanuts has been a folk cultural practice in the southern United States. Peanuts are sometimes called "goober peas."

Black and White Cookie

Ray's Café offers many dessert items. Among them are raspberry coffee cream cheese cake, cinnamon crumble cake, Rice Krispie treats, and the black and white cookie. A black and white cookie is a soft, sponge-cake-like shortbread which is iced on one half with vanilla and on the other half with chocolate. The cookies are often sold in Jewish delis in New York. The black and white cookie was featured in a well-known 1994 episode of the *Seinfeld* television show entitled "The Dinner Party."

TEXAS RANGERS

Globe Life Park in Arlington is located between the cities of Dallas and Fort Worth. The park opened in 1994 and has had multiple names before becoming Globe Life Park just before the 2014 season. The Dallas Cowboys football team also plays in Arlington at nearby AT&T Stadium. Globe Life Park is not roofed and is open to the Texas heat.

Featured Hot Dog/Sausage

The Texas Taco Dog combines the two food classics of hot dogs and tacos. The hot dog is placed inside a taco shell and topped with ground taco meat and traditional taco toppings. The entire taco is then put inside a traditional hot dog bun. It is sold at the Casa de Fuego stand.

Texas Taco Dog

More Hot Dogs and Sausages

The Home Plate Butcher Block serves what is called a Sausage Sundae. The sausage is topped with mashed potatoes, macaroni and cheese, barbequed brisket and a red pickled pepper (which looks like the cherry on top of a sundae).

The Texas Big Dog stand offers three regionally themed foot-long hot dogs. The foot-long Texas Dog comes with chili, cheddar cheese, and grilled onions. The foot-long Big Apple Dog has spicy brown mustard, grilled onions and sauerkraut. The foot-long Chicago Dog comes with pickles, relish, tomato, sport peppers, celery salt and mustard.

The American Dog stand serves a Frito Dog topped with chili, cheese, and Fritos corn chips. The Bacon-Wrapped Dog is wrapped in crispy bacon and smothered in grilled onions. The Bringing the Heat Dog is topped with hot relish, cheddar cheese and jalapeños.

As at the Houston ballpark, all of the beef hot dogs and beef sausages at Globe Life Park are provided by Nolan Ryan All-Natural Beef. In addition to the beef, pork sausages are sold at Globe Life Park. The pork sausages are provided by Earl Campbell Meat Products of Waelder, Texas (south of Austin.) Earl Campbell won the Heisman trophy (college football's highest honor) in 1977 while playing for the University of Texas Longhorns. He then had a long career with the Houston Oilers and was inducted into the Pro-Football Hall of Fame in 1991.

Cholula Hot Wings

Cholula Hot Sauce is a brand of chili-based sauce manufactured in Chapala in the state of Jalisco, Mexico. The recipe, which blends pequin peppers (almost ten times hotter than jalapeños) and red peppers, is a well-guarded secret that is over 100 years old. At Globe Life Park, the Cholula Hot Wing stand offers wing baskets with the signature Cholula Hot Sauce. Wings are also available in barbeque or garlic flavors.

Cholula Hot Wings

Blue Bell Creameries

Blue Bell Creameries is a Texas-based company that also has a stand at Houston's Minute Maid Park. In addition to ice cream cups and cones, the Blue Bell Ice Cream stand at Globe Life Park sells ice cream floats. An ice cream float consists of flavored syrup mixed with ice cream in either a soft drink or carbonated water. The ice cream float was invented by Robert McCay Green in Philadelphia in 1874 during a local celebration. According to a 1910 article in *Soda Fountain Magazine*, Green wanted to create a new treat to attract customers away from another vendor who had a bigger and fancier soda fountain.

Texas Sized 24

It is often said that everything is bigger in Texas. The Texas Sized 24 stand features supersized items that are 24 inches long. Three of them are named for Texas Rangers players.

The Boomstick is a two-foot-long hot dog topped with a layer of chili covered in caramelized onions, a layer of melted jalapeño cheese and jalapeño peppers, served on a potato bun. The hot dog is named for the bat of former Texas Ranger Nelson Cruz. (He moved to the Baltimore Orioles in 2014.) Cruz is known for his long home runs. In a commercial that he did in 2010 for the *MLB 2K10* baseball video game, he called his bat "The Boomstick."

Ka-Boom Kabob

The Choomongous is a two-foot-long Korean barbeque sandwich with chopped beef, spicy slaw, and sriracha mayo on a sweet bun. Sriracha is a chili pepper hot sauce originating in Thailand. The Choomongous is named for Shin-Soo Choo, a Ranger outfielder and native of South Korea. *Dallas Morning News* sports reporter Marcus Murphree decided to eat this sandwich all by himself. He managed to down it in twelve minutes. Murphree said "In baseball speak, this felt like stepping up to the plate and knowing that nothing a pitcher could throw would go by me."

The Ka-Boom Kabob is a two-foot-long shish kabob served on a bed of rice. Pieces of grilled chicken are skewered with cherry tomatoes, peppers, onions and pineapple chunks.

Although not 24 inches long, the Beltre Buster Burger is a one-pound hamburger with bacon, Jack cheese, and grilled onions. The burger is named for third baseman Adrian Beltre who is known for his signature swing of dropping to one knee while belting out a home run.

For fans who want to try a Boomstick or a Choomongous but don't have companions with them to share the supersize serving, mini versions are available at the Right Field Grill.

Totally Rossome Nachos

Totally Rossome Nachos are available at several stands throughout Globe Life Park. The nachos come in a pink souvenir batting helmet and are topped with a choice of brisket or chicken, lettuce, pico de gallo, queso blanco, and sour cream. They are named for pitcher Robbie Ross. Although Ross was sent down to the minors in June of the 2014 season, his nachos remain for sale in the majors.

Smokehouse Mac

Smokehouse 557 serves smoked brisket and turkey sandwiches along with macaroni and cheese. However, the macaroni and cheese is not just a side dish. Both the brisket or the turkey are served on top of the mac and cheese and known as a "Smokehouse Mac."

Smokehouse Mac

Bacon on a Stick

The Home Plate Butcher Block offers Baked Bacon on a Stick, in three variations. Fans can get the bacon covered with a maple glaze, with Old Bay Seasoning or with whipped cream and chocolate syrup.

Frito Pie

Barbeque is provided at the Sweet Baby Ray's stand. Sweet Baby Ray's is a Chicago-based company that sells its barbeque sauces and meats in grocery stores. Barbequed chicken and beef sandwiches, smoked turkey legs, and Frito chili pie (Fritos covered with chili, cheese, and onion) are on the menu there. According to a *Texas Monthly Magazine* article by Michael Hilton, "Frito pies are still a mainstay at football games." Apparently they go well at baseball games as well.

The Chipper

The Chipper stand makes fresh kettle chips. There are four ways to order your Chippers, all of them available with a choice of either chicken or brisket. The Bases Loaded Chipper is topped with nacho cheese, bacon, sour cream and chives. The Southwest Chipper is topped with queso blanco, pico de gallo, and sour cream. The Ballpark BBQ Chipper is topped with barbeque sauce, onions and jalapeños. And lastly, with a Canadian touch, the Texas Poutine Nachos are topped with creamy gravy, bacon, jalapeños, chives and shredded cheddar cheese.

Big Game Pretzel

Big Game Pretzel

Not only do the sandwiches and the kabobs come big in Texas, but fans here can also get a giant pretzel. The Big Game Pretzel is one foot in diameter and comes with nacho cheese, honey mustard, and marinara dipping sauces…a fitting finale to a supersized eating experience.

TORONTO BLUE JAYS

Rogers Centre, originally known as SkyDome, opened in 1989 in downtown Toronto next to the CN Tower. The stadium was the first to have a fully retractable motorized roof. A 348-room hotel is attached. Rogers Centre is also home to the Toronto Argonauts of the Canadian Football League.

Featured Hot Dog/Sausage

The Garrison Creek Foot-Long Hot Dog, an all-beef wiener accompanied by grilled onions and peppers, is officially described by the Blue Jays as their signature hot dog. The hot dog is named for Garrison Creek, a stream that once flowed into Toronto Harbor. It has been largely covered over and filled in, though geographical traces still remain.

Garrison Creek Foot-Long Hot Dog

More Hot Dogs and Sausages

At the Garrison Creek Flat Grill fans can also get a Farmers Sausage. Farmers Sausage is a form of smoked raw pork sausage of Mennonite origin. It is very popular with the Mennonite settlers of southern Ontario and differs from the sausages available in Mennonite communities in the United States.

Shopsy's Deli

Shopsy's Deli, known as the "King of Sandwiches" since the early 1920s, was opened in Toronto in 1921 by Harry Shopsowitz and his wife Jenny. The couple ran their restaurant until Harry died in 1945, and the business was passed on to their sons, Sam and Izzy. Sam and Izzy decided to expand the business in 1947 by opening a meat processing plant. The restaurant, although no longer owned by the Shopsowitz family, remains a Toronto institution. The meat processing business was sold in 1992 to Maple Leaf Foods.

Montreal Smoked Meat Sandwich

Shopsy's at Rogers Centre offers a Montreal Smoked Meat Sandwich. Montreal-style smoked meat is made by salting and curing beef brisket with spices for at least a week, and then smoking and steaming the meat. Warm Montreal-smoked meat is always sliced by hand since a meat slicer would cause the tender meat to disintegrate. The sandwich is traditionally served on rye bread with mustard.

Also available are pastrami sandwiches, corned beef sandwiches, and the Bill Cosby Triple Decker Sandwich (pastrami and corned beef with three pieces of bread.) Actor and comedian Bill Cosby is a big fan of Shopsy's.

Sunflower Seeds

Sunflower seeds have become popular with baseball players. Traditionally ballplayers chewed tobacco but as the harmful effects of tobacco became known, many players switched to sunflower seeds. By the 1980s, the seeds had surpassed tobacco in on-field popularity. This popularity spread to the fans in the stands, and soon sunflower seeds were competing with peanuts. Rogers Centre sells Spitz Sunflower Seeds. In 1982 Alberta family farmers Tom and Emmy Droog decided to switch from planting wheat to sunflowers, and established Spitz Sunflower Seeds. Their small business kept growing until it was sold to Frito-Lay in 2008.

Hall of Famer Chicken Wrap

#12 Roberto Alomar

The 12 Kitchen is named in honor of former Toronto Blue Jay infielder Roberto Alomar, who wore jersey number 12. Alomar was the first Toronto Blue Jay to be inducted into the National Baseball Hall of Fame. The 12 Kitchen serves the Hall of Famer Chicken Wrap. A spinach tortilla is filled with spiced fire-roasted chicken, crushed cilantro mojo, romaine hearts, chorizo crackle, Asiago cheese and Caesar dressing.

#12 Nachos

The 12 Nachos use homestyle kettle potato chips instead of tortilla chips. The chips are topped with warm cheddar cheese, sliced Canadian peameal bacon, charred corn and pineapple salsa, diced red tomatoes, shredded pickles, and jalapeño-infused island sauce. Peameal bacon is a type of bacon that originated in Toronto. The name reflects the historic practice of rolling the cured meat in dried and ground yellow peas. Today it is rolled in yellow cornmeal instead.

Poutine

Poutine

Poutine is a Canadian dish originating in Quebec. French fries are topped with a light brown gravy and cheese curds. The dish is now popular in all parts of Canada as well as some places in the northern United States. The Hog Town Grill serves traditional poutine at Rogers Centre.

The Quaker Steak and Lube stand serves a version of poutine known as Wedge & Wing Poutine. Potato wedges and chunks of breaded chicken are combined with blue cheese dressing and nacho cheese. The stand also serves fish tacos made with tilapia.

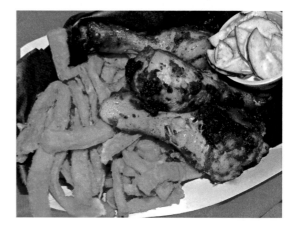

Adobo Chicken Trio

Muddy York

An early and disparaging nickname for Toronto was "Muddy York." At the time there were no storm drains and the streets were unpaved. During rainfall, water would accumulate on the dirt roads, transforming them into impassable muddy avenues. Two of the stands at Rogers Centre use the Muddy York name.

The Muddy York Market serves various specialities including a Little Italy Meatball Hoagie, a Big Smoke Jerk Chicken Sandwich, a Distillery Beef Brisket Sandwich, and the Adobo Chicken Trio. The Adobo Chicken Trio consists of three barbequed chicken drumsticks cooked "adobo" style. The raw chicken is immersed in a sauce composed of paprika, oregano, salt, garlic, and vinegar to preserve and enhance its flavor. This practice is native to Iberia, Spain.

The Muddy York Cantina offers a five-step "Create Your Own Cantina Box." Step 1: Choose your base (tortilla chips, burrito, or romaine lettuce). Step 2: Choose your starter (warm cheddar cheese, three-bean chili, black beans, fresh pico de gallo or cantina rice). Step 3: Choose your topping (jerk chicken, smoked chopped pork, barbeque beef brisket; vegetarians can choose a second item from Step 2). Step 4: Choose up to four favorite market ingredients (salsa verde, red cabbage slaw, roasted corn salsa, pico de gallo, green onions, sun-dried tomatoes, jalapeños, black olives, guacamole, chili lime sour cream, or sautéed peppers and onions). Step 5: "Enjoy your cantina box!"

Craft Chop House Burger

Fresh Burger offers a Craft Chop House Burger and invites fans to "make it your own." There is a wide variety of sauces and cold and hot toppings, advertised as over 6,500 possible combinations. (In the interest of space, I won't list all 6,500 choices.)

Cavendish Farms

Potatoes can be found at various stands at Rogers Centre. They come in the form of poutine, regular French fries, curly fries, and fries with various toppings. Many ballparks have an official hot dog, but Rogers Centre also has an official potato provider. Cavendish Farms, located on Prince Edward Island, provides all the potatoes throughout the stadium. In 2001 Cavendish Farms became the first frozen potato processing company to switch all their products to non-hydrogenated oil. It sells over one billion pounds of potatoes annually.

WASHINGTON NATIONALS

The Nationals Park is located along the Anacostia River in the Navy Yard neighborhood of Washington, DC. The stadium opened in 2008 as the new home of the Nationals, who had played at RFK Stadium after their move from Montreal to Washington in 2005.

Featured Hot Dog/Sausage

Ben's Chili Bowl serves its well-known Original Half-Smoke. Ben and Virginia Ali opened Ben's Chili Bowl in 1958. They renovated the Minnehaha Theater, which first housed silent movies in 1910. Ten days before his inauguration in 2009, President-Elect Barack Obama visited and ate lunch there.

Half-Smoke

A half-smoke is similar to a hot dog but spicier and made with more coarsely-ground meat. The hot dog, made from half pork and half beef combined with herbs, onions, and chili sauce, is smoked slowly. At Nationals Park, the Original Half-Smoke is served "all the way" accompanied by chili, cheese, onions, and mustard.

More Hot Dogs and Sausages

The Grand Slam Grill serves the DMV. I spent the evening wondering why a hot dog would be named for the Department of Motor Vehicles. My research discovered that DMV refers to the DC metro area and stands for DC, Maryland, and Virginia. The DMV is a foot-long half-smoke (from DC) smothered with Maryland crab dip and topped with Virginia ham.

Senator Sausages serves bratwurst, Italian sausages, and andouille sausages. Andouille sausage, of French origin, is most often associated with Acadians and Cajun cooking of Louisiana.

All-beef Hebrew National hot dogs are available at Nationals Park. Hebrew National Kosher Sausage Factory was founded by a Russian immigrant, Theodore Krainin, in 1905 in the Lower East Side of Manhattan. In the 1940s, the company created products especially for grocery stores and the suburban market. Its products appeal to all consumers and not just to those who keep kosher.

Shawafel

The Shawafel stand at Nationals Park serves many of the same Lebanese specialties that local customers will find at their H Street restaurant location of the same name. Its name comes from the combination of two popular Middle Eastern foods, shawarma and falafel. Shawarma is meat slow-cooked on a vertical spit for many hours. Shavings are cut off the block of meat. Falafel is a deep-fried ball or patty made from ground spiced chickpeas and/or fava beans. Shawarma and falafel are commonly served in a pita bread pocket or wrap.

At Nationals Park, the Shawafel stand serves chicken or lamb and beef shawarma. The falafel is made from chick peas. Both are served in pita pockets with tahini sauce made from ground sesame seeds. Also served is a Cauliflower Sandwich Wrap made with fried cauliflower, parsley, lettuce, tomatoes, pickles and tahini sauce. Side dishes include Baba Ghanoush, Lebanese Fries and Hummus. Baba Ghanoush is a puree made from eggplant and sesame paste. The eggplant is peeled and mashed, then mixed with sesame paste, garlic, salt, pepper, cumin, lemon juice and olive oil. Lebanese Fries are French fries topped with zaatar (also referred to as za'atar), a spice mixture made with dried herbs including marjoram, thyme, oregano, sumac, cumin, and sesame seeds. Hummus is a puree of chickpeas, garlic, tahini and lemon juice.

Cauliflower Sandwich Wrap

Italian Hero

G by Mike Isabella

Chef Mike Isabella opened G Sandwich Shop next to his Northern Greek restaurant, Kapnos, along the 14th Street corridor in Washington, DC. At Nationals Park, G by Mike Isabella serves four of his gourmet sandwiches. The Chicken Parm sandwich has chicken thigh ragu, provolone, and Thai basil. The Italian Hero has capicola (an Italian cold cut made from the pork shoulder or neck), soppressata (Italian dry salami), prosciutto, mozzarella, oil and vinegar, mayonnaise, and pickled vegetables. The Roasted Cauliflower sandwich has almond romesco (a Catalan condiment made with almonds, roasted tomatoes, olive oil and vinegar), pickled vegetables, and paprika. The Drewno sandwich is named for Scott Drewno, the executive chef at The Source restaurant in the Newseum in Washington, DC. The Drewno has kielbasa sausage, roast beef, and sauerkraut.

Dolci Gelati

Dolci Gelati sells gelato throughout the Washington, DC area. The company was founded in 2006 by pastry chef Gianluigi Dellaccio, who uses ingredients from local dairy farms and fruit orchards. Its chocolate is imported from a small sustainable farm in Ecuador. Flavors available at Nationals Park are chocolate, cookies and cream, stracciatella (chocolate chip), baccio (chocolate hazelnut), peanut butter, strawberry, lemon, and mango.

Teddy Roosevelt Cupcake

Fluffy Thoughts Bakery was founded by Lara Stuckey, combining her two passions of art and baking. Her stand at Nationals Park sells brownies, cookies, and cupcakes. What would be more appropriate in Washington, DC, than a presidential cupcake? The Teddy Roosevelt Cupcake has a salted caramel ganache filling and vanilla frosting. Teddy's glasses are made of hard icing, and he has a chocolate moustache.

Teddy Roosevelt Cupcake

Union Square Hospitality Group

New York restaurateur Danny Meyer's Union Square Hospitality Group has four stands at New York's Citi Field. These four – Shake Shack, Box Frites, Blue Smoke Barbeque, and El Verano Taqueria – are also found at Nationals Park.

Chesapeake Crab Cake Specialties

Chesapeake Crab Cake Specialties serves jumbo lump crab cakes with mixed greens, tomatoes, and Old Bay remoulade. (Remoulade, invented in France, is similar to tartar sauce. It is mayonnaise based and can be flavored with curry, horseradish, paprika, anchovies, or other items.) Fans can also get a crab grilled cheese sandwich on sourdough bread with Brie. Homemade tortilla chips are served with crab queso and corn cilantro salsa.

Change Up Chicken

The Change Up Chicken stand features chicken in a waffle cone. Pieces of chicken are breaded with waffle crumbs, then served in an ice cream cone.

Field of Greens

The Field of Greens serves a wide variety of vegetarian options, greater than what is found in most ballparks. Its menu includes vegan crab cakes, grilled portobello sandwich, grilled veggie wrap, veggie cheese steak, veggie hot dog, house made veggie burger, and a variety of meatless salads.

Taste of the Majors

The Taste of the Majors offers foods from other parts of the country including the Miami Cuban Sandwich, the Arizona Quesadilla, and the New York Pastrami Sandwich.

Jammin' Island BBQ

The Jammin' Island BBQ serves Caribbean food. Jerk chicken and jerk ribs are accompanied by rice and beans, plantains, and yucca fries. Yucca is a desert plant grown in arid sections of North America.

Intentional Wok

The Intentional Wok features Chicken Pad Thai Noodles and Beef Drunken Noodles. Asian vegetables mixed with soy sauce, eggs, and diced peanuts complement the Chicken Pad Thai Noodles. The Beef Drunken Noodles has beef mixed with Asian vegetables and a Thai basil sauce.

Crab Pretzel

Pretzels come in many varieties at Nationals Park. The Pretzel Loaf is a pretzel stuffed with steak and cheese. The Half-Smoke Pretzel Log is -- you guessed it -- a half-smoke hot dog inside a pretzel. Finally, the Crab Pretzel is an oblong twisted pretzel topped with large amounts of a crab meat mixture.

Crab Pretzel

If you are reading this now you have just survived a culinary tour of the 30 MLB ballparks without gaining a pound—something my wife and I can not truthfully say.

The new food era has brought such a wonderful gustatory experience at the ballparks with chef-prepared masterpieces, vegetarian and kosher delights, as well as amped up riffs on the hot dog and sausage.

While it is unlikely that food choices and prices will revert to the simpler fare of the early days of baseball during the Harry M. Stevens era, we can still celebrate and remember the beginning of the food-baseball connection—a firmly entrenched connection that is here to stay.

SOURCES

Notes:

    All websites were accessed between January and October of 2014.

    Background information was also obtained from restaurants and food purveyors.

"27 Reasons Deep Dish Pizza is Better Than All Other Pizzas." *BuzzFeed.* www.buzzfeed.com

"Adobo." *Food Network: Food Encyclopedia.* www.foodterms.com

"Adrian Beltre Biography." *JockBio.* www.jockbio.com

Agha-Ghassem, Payam. "2014 National Hot Dog Day." *Baltimore Magazine*, 15 Jul. 2014.

"Albert Von Tilzer, Tin Pan Alley Pioneer." *The Parlor Songs Academy.* www.parlorsongs.com

"All About Wild Rice." *Whole Grains Council.* www.wholegrainscouncil.org

Allen, Scott. "9 Famous Baseball Stadium Vendors." *mental_floss.* www.mentalfloss.com

"America's Favorite Sweet Onion." *The Vidalia Onion Committee.* www.vidaliaonion.org

"Amusement Business Spotlights 100th Anniversary of Harry M. Stevens Inc." *Amusement Business*, 1 Aug. 1987.

Anderson, Jean. *The American Century Cookbook: The Most Popular Recipes of the 20th Century.* New York: Gramercy Books, 2005.

"Angus." *Oklahoma State University Department of Animal Science.* www.ansi.okstate.edu

Armour, Mark. "Luis Tiant." *Society for American Baseball Research.* www.sabr.org

Armour, Mark. "Willie McCovey." *Society for American Baseball Research.* www.sabr.org

"Atlantic City Baseball Club Scorecard 1896." [Obtained from the National Baseball Hall of Fame]

"Authentic Philly Cheesesteaks." *Visit Philadelphia.* www.visitphilly.com

"The Authorship Debate." *Shakespeare Resource Center.* www.bardweb.net

Avey, Tori. "Discover the History of Chicken and Waffles." *PBS.* www.pbs.org

"Baba Ghanouj." *Food History.* www.world-foodhistory.com

"Ballpark Food Continues to Upscale." *Food Management.* www.food-management.com

"Bao and Mantou." *Chinatownology.* www.chinatownology.com

"Baseball Hall of Fame Honors Harry Stevens Family, Caterers." *Post-Star* [Glens Falls, NY], 20 Sep. 1978.

"Baseball's Love Affair With Food." *NBC 7 San Diego.* www.nbc7.com

Bearak, Barry. "A Passion to Pitch: Yankees' Masahiro Tanaka Epitomizes the Japanese Approach to Baseball." *New York Times*, 29 Mar. 2014.

Beaton, Rod. "Buy Me Some Pierogies and Kosher Dogs." *USA Today,* 16 Apr. 2001.

"Beignets: From Scriblita to the Big Easy." *National Geographic.* www.education.nationalgeographic.com

Bellis, Mary. "The History of TV Dinners." *About.* www.about.com

"Best Ballpark Foods." *USA Weekend*, 21 Mar. 2014.

"Best Baseball Stadium Food." *Men's Journal.* www.mensjournal.com

Bethune, Meredith. "What's the Difference Between Tex-Mex and Mexican Food?" *Serious Eats.* www.seriouseats.com

Bickley, Dan. "The American Dream Alive and Well at Chase Field." *The Arizona Republic*, 15 Jun. 2014.

Biederman, Les. "Foodman O'Brisky a 40-Year Landmark Around Pirate Park." *Pittsburgh Press*, 22 Jun. 1968.

SOURCES

"Bio." *Frank Viola.* www.frankviolabaseball.com

"Birthplace of the Hot Dog." *What's Cooking America.* www.whatscookingamerica.net

Bjarkman, Peter C. "Tony Oliva." *Society for American Baseball Research.* www.sabr.org

"Black and White Cookies." *Smitten Kitchen.* www.smittenkitchen.com

"Boiled Peanuts." *What's Cooking America.* www.whatscookingamerica.net

Bonwich, Joe. "What's a Knish? Kosher Stand Draws a Crowd at Busch." *St. Louis Post-Dispatch*, 7 Jul. 2013.

Boo, James. "What are Burnt Ends? And Why are They So Delicious?" *Serious Eats.* www.seriouseats.com

Boyer, Rona. "Food and Drink." *Millbrook* [NY] *Independent*, 9 Oct. 2013.

Bradley, Hugh. "$700 Started Stevens to Hot Dog Millions." *New York Journal-American*, 20 Aug. 1960.

Branch, John. "An Old Reliable at the Old Ball Game." *New York Times*, 14 Oct. 2009.

"Bratwurst." *German Food Guide.* www.germanfoodguide.com

"A Brief History of Natural Casings." *International Natural Sausage Casing Association.* www.insca.org

Brokaw, Sanford. "The Peanut Man Connie Mack Hired." *Philadelphia Inquirer*, 13 Oct. 1974.

Browning-Bals, Kristen. "Ellerbee's Looking Forward to Next Bite." *Denver Post*, 11 May 2005.

Buckley, J. Taylor. "Hot Dog Vendors Know Baseball's Real Meaning." *USA Today*, 19 Feb. 1998.

"Bul-Go-Gi: Grilled Marinated Beef." TriFood. *Celebrating Korean Food.* www.trifood.com

Burnette, Margarette. "Summer's New Twist: Pretzel Bread Takes Off as Customers Look for Premium Choices." *QSR Magazine*, Jul. 2013.

"Candy History and Lore; Chocolate Turtles." *Candy Turtle.* www.candyturtle.com

"Capocollo." *Food Network: Food Encyclopedia.* www.foodterms.com

Chabot, Hillary. "Mitt Romney's Grits and Catfish Act Goes Too Far for Southern Critics." *Boston Herald*, 13 Mar. 2012.

Chapman, Francesca. "Aramark Swallows Harry M. Stevens." *Philadelphia Inquirer*, 13 Dec. 1994.

"Chef Roberto Santibañez." *Delish.* www.delish.com

"Chimichurri." *Cambalache's Gourmet.* www.cambalachesla.com

"Churros: The Hidden History." *Huffington Post.* www.huffingtonpost.com

"Cleveland's Great Mustard Debate." *All Things Cleveland Ohio.* www.allthingsclevelandohio.blogspot.com

Code of Federal Regulations. Washington, DC: U.S. Government Printing Office, 2014.

Cohen, Gerald Leonard, Barry A. Popik, and David Shulman. *Origin of the Term 'Hot Dog.'* Rolla, MO: Gerald Cohen, 2004.

Collins, Gail. "'Hot Dog,' This Company Says, After Being in Business Almost 100 Years." *Los Angeles Times*, 15 Jan. 1985.

"Coney Dog Recipe at Comerica Park." *Sportscierge.* www.sportscierge.com

Corn, Elaine. "Fans' Fare: Expanding the Classics of Baseball." *The Courier-Journal* [Louisville, KY], 14 Apr. 1982.

"Cracker Jack." *About.* www.about.com

"Cretors History." *Cretors.* www.cretors.com

"Dachsunds, Dog Wagons and Other Important Elements of Hot Dog History." *National Hot Dog and Sausage Council.* www.hot-dog.org

Danze, Tina. "Mexican Street Food is Hot; How To Do It Yourself at Home." *Dallas Morning News*, 4 Sep. 2012.

Deal, Chad. "Burrito Barato: Surfin' California at Lucha Libre." *San Diego Reader*, 16 Jul. 2011.

"Derby's Claim to the Hot Dog: Is a Derby Man the Real Inventor of the Best-Selling Sausage Snack?"
BBC. www.bbc.co.uk

Dewey, Donald. *The 10th Man: The Fan in Baseball History.* New York: Carroll & Graf, 2004.

Dickson, Paul. *The New Dickson Baseball Dictionary: A Cyclopedic Reference to More Than 7,000 Words, Names,*

Phrases, and Slang Expressions That Define the Game, Its Heritage, Culture, and Variations.
New York: Harcourt Brace & Co., 1999.

"Difference Between Sausage and Hot Dog."
Difference Between Similar Terms and Objects. www.differencebetween.net

Diggs, Lisa. "100 Years of Smooth Sailing for Sanders Bumpy Cake." *Buy Michigan Now.* www.buymichigannow.com

"The Dinner Party." *Seinfeld Scripts.* www.seinfeldscripts.com

"Dizzy Dean." *National Baseball Hall of Fame.* www.baseballhall.org

"DMV." *Urban Dictionary.* www.urbandictionary.com

Dougherty, Steve. "What a Long, Strange Trip." *People*, 21 Aug. 1995.

Dycus, John. "'Birdman' of Pennants." *Fort Worth Star-Telegram*, 30 Jun. 1974.

"Earl Campbell." *Pro Football Hall of Fame.* www.profootballhof.com

"The Economy of Food at Sporting Events."
Sports Management Degree Guide. www.sports-management-degrees.com

"Elk Meat." *North American Elk Breeders Association.* www.naelk.org

Elkies, Lauren. "Danny Meyer." *The Real Deal: New York City Real Estate News.* www.therealdeal.com

"Elysian Fields." *Project Ballpark.* www.projectballpark.org

Enders, Deborah G. "Food Service Keeps Pace With Changing Tastes." *Amusement Business*, 7 Mar. 1994.

Engel, Jeff. "Milwaukee Brewers Mascot Gets Own Themed Beer." *Milwaukee Business Journal*, 22 May 2013.

"English-Born Creator of Hot Dog Dies at 78." *Washington Post*, 5 May 1934.

Eskenazi, Gerald. "Hero or Grinder or Sub, Sports Food is Big Time." *New York Times*, 10 Mar. 1974.

"Etymology of Hot Dog." *Snopes: Rumor Has It.* www.snopes.com

"An Explanation of Our Company Name." *Muddy York Walking Tours.* www.muddyyorktours.com

"Exploring Constitutional Conflicts: Regulation of Obscenity."
University of Missouri-Kansas City School of Law. www.law.umkc.edu

"FAQs About Curds." *Wisconsin Milk Marketing Board.* www.eatcurds.com

Fernandez, Manny. "Buy Me Some Peanuts and Nectarines." *New York Times*, 29 Aug. 2009.

"Field of Dreams." *Field of Dreams Movie Site.* www.fodmoviesite.com

"Food & Think: The Updated History of Baseball Stadium Nachos." *Smithsonian Magazine*, 7 May 2013.

Fost, Dan. *Giants Past & Present.* 2nd ed. Minneapolis: MVP Books, 2011.

Foster, John B. *Spalding's Official Baseball Guide 1913.* Reprint ed. Whitefish, MT: Kessinger Publishing, 2004.

Frederick, Missy. "Stadium Food Vendors Concede Profits are No Slam Dunk, but the Branding is Unbeatable."
Washington Business Journal, 30 Mar. 2012.

"Fun Facts." *National Peanut Board.* www.nationalpeanutboard.org

Galuten, Noah. "Evolution of the Dodger Dog." *LA Weekly*, 21 Aug. 2009.

"Ganache." *iFood.* www.ifood.tv

"Garlic Fries: The Story." *Gordon Biersch.* www.gordonbiersch.com

"The Gashouse Gang Wins the World Series." *History.* www.history.com

SOURCES

"Go-Chu-Jang: Korean Chili Pepper Paste." *TriFood*: Celebrating Korean Food. www.trifood.com

"Gorman Thomas." *Historic Baseball*. www.historicbaseball.com

Green, Daniel S. *The Perfect Pitch: The Biography of Roger Owens, the Famous Peanut Man at Dodger Stadium*. Coral Springs, FL: Llumina Press, 2004.

"Greg Luzinski Biography." *The Baseball Page*. www.thebaseballpage.com

"Guide to Sweet Riesling Wine." *Total Wine*. www.totalwine.com

"A Guide to the Jewish Delis of Los Angeles." *First We Feast*. www.firstwefeast.com

Hainer, Cathy. "Ballparks Pitching More Than Hot Dogs to Hungry Fans." *USA Today*, 7 Jun. 1994.

Hall, Trish. "New Yankee Call: Getcha Fresh Shrimp!" *New York Times*, 17 May 1988.

"Hampton Farms & Major League Baseball." *Hampton Farms*. www.hamptonfarms.com

"Harry M. Stevens." *New York Historical Society*. www.nyhistory.org

"Harry M. Stevens." *Ohio History Central*. www.ohiohistorycentral.org

"Harry M. Stevens Dies at Age of 78." *New York Times*, 4 May 1934.

The Harry M. Stevens Family Foundation. *Harry M. Stevens Inc.: 1887-1994*. New York: The Harry M. Stevens Family Foundation, 1995.

"Healthy Eats at 30 Major League Baseball Parks." *Health Magazine*. www.health.com

"The Heavenly Appeal of Moon Pies." *NPR*. www.npr.org

Hetrick, J. Thomas. *Chris Von der Ahe and the St. Louis Browns*. Lanham, MD: Scarecrow Press, 1999.

Hevesi, Dennis. "Morrie Yohai, 90, the Man Behind Cheez Doodles, is Dead." *New York Times*, 2 Aug. 2010.

Hilton, Michael. "Texas Primer: Frito Pie." *Texas Monthly*, Nov. 1986.

Hiskey, Daven. "Why Are Potatoes Called Spuds?" *mental_floss*. www.mentalfloss.com

"History of Falafel." *Food History*. www.world-foodhistory.com

"The History of Goetta." *Kitchen Project*. www.kitchenproject.com

"History of Hoagies, Submarine Sandwiches, Po' Boys Sandwiches, Dagwood Sandwiches, & Italian Sandwiches." *What's Cooking America*. www.whatscookingamerica.net

"A History of Kansas City-Style Barbeque." *Kansas City Convention & Visitors Association*. www.visitkc.com

"History of Maryland Crab Soup." *Mid-Atlantic Cooking*. www.midatlanticcooking.wordpress.com

"History of Reuben Sandwich." *What's Cooking America*. www.whatscookingamerica.net

"History of Salads and Salad Dressings." *What's Cooking America*. www.whatscookingamerica.net

"Hot Dog! This Idea's a Natural." *Cooperstown Crier* [Cooperstown, NY], 25 Jan. 2001.

"Hot Dog: Polo Grounds Myth." *The Big Apple*. www.barrypopik.com

"Hot Dogs and Food Safety." *United States Department of Agriculture. Food Safety and Inspection Service*. www.fsis.usda.gov

"Hot Dogs are Frankly a Home Run Hit With Baseball Fans." *National Hot Dog and Sausage Council*. www.hot-dog.org

"Hot Dogs at Baseball Games." *The Big Apple*. www.barrypopik.com

"The House That Ruth Built." *The Official Family Site of George Herman "Babe" Ruth*. www.thetruebaberuth.com

Huff, Andrew. "Neon Green Relish." *Gapers Block*. www.gapersblock.com

Hurte, Bob. "Manny Sanguillen." *Society for American Baseball Research*. www.sabr.org

"Ignacio Anaya: The Real Inventor of Nachos." *Huffington Post*. www.huffingtonpost.com

Isaacson, Melissa. "A Vendor's Farewell." *Chicago Tribune*, 26 Nov. 1995.

Isella, Elena. "Scott Drewno's 'Source' of Passion for Asian Cuisine." *Fox News*. www.foxnews.com

"It's 1, 2, 3 Strikes and Out for Trans Fats in Many Ballparks." *Kansas City Star*, 21 Mar. 2007.

"Jack Norworth Exhibit." *Songwriters Hall of Fame*. www.songwritershalloffame.org

Jackson, Donald Dale. "Hot Dogs are Us." *Smithsonian Magazine*, June 1999.

Jay, Ben. "What's the Difference Between Pastrami and Montreal Smoked Meat?" *Serious Eats*. www.seriouseats.com

Kaplan, Ron. "The Story of Baseball's 'Designated Hebrew.'" *New Jersey Jewish News*, Apr. 2006.

"Kashrut: Jewish Dietary Laws." *Judaism 101*. www.jewfaq.org

"Keith Hernandez Biography." *The Baseball Page*. www.thebaseballpage.com

Kenyon, Chelsie. "Barbacoa." *About*. www.about.com

Kerlin, Janet. "Stuffing Your Face at Games Just Got Easier." *Albany* [NY] *Times Union*, 19 Oct. 1997.

"Kim-Chi: Fermented Cabbage." *TriFood: Celebrating Korean Food*. www.trifood.com

Kindelsperger, Nick. "Taste Test: The Best Hot Giardiniera." *Serious Eats*. www.chicago.seriouseats.com

King, Mary, and Jean Meadows. "Florida Food Fare."
University of Florida, Sarasota County Extension. www.sarasota.ifas.ufl.edu

King, Paul. "Harry M. Stevens." *Nation's Restaurant News*, Feb. 1996.

King, Paul. "Out to the Ballgame." *FoodService Director*, 15 Sep. 2007.

Klein, Michael. "Now There's Takeout Out at the Ball Game." *Philadelphia Inquirer*, 23 Sep. 2010.

Kraig, Bruce. *Hot Dog: A Global History*. London: Reakiton Books, 2009.

Krall, Hawk. "Hot Dog of the Week: Cincinnati Cheese Coney." *Serious Eats*. www.seriouseats.com

LaHuta, David. "Best Baseball Stadium Food." *Travel & Leisure*, May 2009.

Laudan, Rachel. *The Food of Paradise: Exploring Hawaii's Culinary Heritage*.
Honolulu: University of Hawaii Press, 1996.

Lazarus, George. "Frito-Lay Wins Cracker Jack." *Chicago Tribune*, 9 Oct. 1997.

Lefton, Brad. "A Baseball Bun-anza." *St. Louis Post-Dispatch*, 8 Jun. 1996.

Lewis, Hunter. "Za'atar." *Bon Appétit*, Jul. 2011.

Lewis, Jill. "Restaurants: Diner's Minneapple Pie is a Hit at Target Field."
Vita.mn: The Twin Cities Going Out Guide. www.vita.mn

Lieb, Fred. [Interview with Harry Stevens.] *The Sporting News*, 18 Nov. 1926.

Lindberg, Richard. *White Sox Encyclopedia*. Philadelphia: Temple University Press, 1997.

Lopata, Peg. "Traditions of the Game." *Cobblestone*, Apr. 2010.

López-Alt, J. Kenji. "How To Make Mexican Street Corn (Elotes)." *Serious Eats*. www.seriouseats.com

Lorin, Janet Frankston. "Hot Dog! Kosher Finding Knish on Sports Venue Menus." *Tucson Citizen*, 29 Nov. 2006.

"Maine House Votes for Whoopie Pie as State Treat." Bangor Daily News, 23 Mar. 2011.

"Making Concessions to Customers' Tastes." *Chronicle-Telegram* [Elyria, OH], 22 Sep. 1996.

Mallett, Chris. "Hot Dog Seller Harry Stevens Remembered With Blue Plaque."
Derby Telegraph [Derby, UK], 12 Feb. 2013.

"Marge Schott Biography." *Famous Sports Stars*. www.sports.jrank.org

Mariani, John *The Encyclopedia of American Food and Drink*. New York: Bloomsbury, 2013.

Mariani, John. "The Secret Origins of the Bloody Mary." *Esquire*, 21 Feb. 2014.

McCafferty, Gratton. "A Caterer With Millions of Customers." *The American Magazine*, 1916.

SOURCES

McDaniel, Douglas. "Man Bites Dog! Great Moments in Hot Dog History." *The Diamond*, Aug. 1993.

McGarry, Tim. "Padres Win the Stadium Food King Challenge." *USA Today*, 17 Jul. 2013.

"Meet Andrew Zimmern." *Travel Channel*. www.travelchannel.com

Mercuri, Becky. *Great American Hot Dog Book: Recipes and Side Dishes from Across America.*
Salt Lake City: Gibbs Smith, 2007.

Miller, Perry. "How to Cook and Serve Yucca Root." *SFGate*. www.sfgate.com

Miller, Richard K. and Kelli Washington. *Sports Marketing 2013.*
Loganville, GA: Richard K. Miller & Associates, 2012.

"Montreal Poutine History." *Montreal Poutine*. www.montrealpoutine.com

Murphree, Marcus. "The Choomongous is a 24-Inch Korean-Themed Foodie's Nightmare, but Hey, There's Veggies on It." *Dallas Morning News*, 15 Apr. 2014.

"National Cheese Doodle Day." *Punchbowl*. www.punchbowl.com

"New York Steak Definition." *Epicurious*. www.epicurious.com

Newman, Mark. "Ballpark Fare So Much More Than Dogs, Peanuts: Food Choices Around the Big Leagues Offer Great Variety and Taste." *MLB*. www.mlb.com

Newman, Mark. "Ode to the Hot Dog." *MLB*. www.mlb.com

Newport, Frank. "In U.S., 5% Consider Themselves Vegetarians." *Gallup*. www.gallup.com

Nichols, Ann. "The Waffle House." *One for the Table*. www.oneforthetable.com

"The Nine Secrets of Stadium Snacking." *Life*, 9 Oct. 2004.

"Nolan Ryan Biography." *Biography*. www.biography.com

"North Beach—San Francisco Travel." *SFGate*. www.sfgate.com

Nyerges, Christopher. "Guide to Edible Seaweed." *Mother Earth News*. www.motherearthnews.com

"Obesity and Overweight." *Centers for Disease Control and Prevention*. www.cdc.gov

"The Original 'Schmitter' Sandwich." *CBS Philly*. philadelphia.cbslocal.com

"Outcry Forces Yanks to Bring Back Cracker Jack." *New York Times*, 2 Jun. 2004.

Pahigian, Josh, and Kevin O'Connell. *Ultimate Baseball Road Trip: A Fan's Guide to Major League Stadiums.* Guilford, CT: Globe Pequot Press, 2nd ed., 2012.

Patterson, Arthur E. (Red). "Stevens Family, Caterers to Fans, Sold First Hot Dog on a Cold Day Hunch at Polo Grounds, 40 Years Ago." *New York Herald Tribune*, 23 Nov. 1939.

Peanut Advisory Board. *History of an All-Star in a Nutshell.* [press release; date unknown]

"Peanut Allergy." *Asthma and Allergy Foundation of America*. www.aafa.org

"Pecans." *Agricultural Marketing Resource Center*. www.agmrc.org

Pellegrini, Megan. "Concessions Play Ball! Sports Stadium Vendors are Finding Success Offering Bold, Ethnic Flavors and Healthy Options." *The National Provisioner*, Sep. 2007.

Peta, Joe. *Trading Bases: A Story About Wall Street, Gambling, and Baseball (Not Necessarily in that Order).*
New York: Dutton, 2013.

"Peter Cavagnaro." *beta blook. BAM/PFA*. blook.bampfa.berkeley.edu

"Pit Beef." *Serious Eats*. www.seriouseats.com

"Polish Hill." *Pittsburgh City Living!* www.pittsburghcityliving.com

"Pork Cuts: The Different Cuts of Ribs and Pork." *Amazingribs*. www.amazingribs.com

"Pretzels." *German Food Guide*. www.germanfoodguide.com

"Randy Jones." *Baseball Library*. www.baseballlibrary.com

Reinhart, Peter. "Marble Rye Bread." *Fine Cooking*, Feb. 2014.

"Remesco Sauce." *Life Café*. www.lifecafe.com

"Restaurateur Award: Chef Ethan Stowell." *StarChefs*. www.starchefs.com

Restivo, Danny. "Niles Man Invented Ballpark Treats, Traditions." *Youngstown [OH] Vindicator*, 21 Apr. 2013.

Reynolds, Quentin. "Peanut Vender." *Colliers Magazine*, 19 Oct. 1935.

Rich, Frank. "Theater: 'Diamonds,' A Revue About Baseball." *New York Times*, 17 Dec. 1984.

Rippon, Nicola. *Derbyshire's Own*. Gloucestershire, UK: Sutton Publishing, 2006.

"Robbie Ross: Biography and Facts." *Whoislog*. www.whoislog.info

"Roberto Alomar." *National Baseball Hall of Fame*. www.baseballhall.org

Rodriguez, Douglas. *The Great Ceviche Book*. Rev. ed. Berkeley, CA: Ten Speed Press, 2010.

Ross, John. "Old Ball Game." *Columbus Monthly*, Sep. 2012.

Rujikarn, Sherry. "The 5 Hottest Trends in Snack Foods." *Good Housekeeping*, 19 Apr. 2013.

Rushin, Steve. *The 34-Ton Bat: The Story of Baseball as Told Through Bobbleheads, Cracker Jacks, Jockstraps, Eye Black, and 375 Other Strange and Unforgettable Objects*. New York: Little, Brown, 2013.

Sabo, John N. "Hot Dogs." *Allsports Magazine*, July 1945.

Sacks, Katherine and Will Blunt. "The Product: Porchetta, Digging Into Italian Culinary History." *StarChefs*. www.starchefs.com

"San Francisco Restaurant Guide: Chinatown." *Coast News*. www.coastnews.com

Schultz, E.J. "From Hot Dogs to Sushi, The Greatest Moments in Baseball-Park Food History." *Advertising Age*, 12 Jul. 2012.

Segal, David. "The Gyro's History Unfolds." *New York Times*, 14 Jul. 2009.

Sharrow, Ryan. "Ballpark Smorgasbord." *Baltimore Business Journal*, 30 Jul. 2007.

"Shin-Soo Choo: Biography and Facts." *Whoislog*. www.whoislog.info

Shvorin, Vladimir. "Fenway Park Adds Kosher Hot Dogs." *Jewish Advocate*, 14 Apr. 2008.

Silver, Laura. *Knish: In Search of the Jewish Soul Food*. Waltham, MA: Brandeis University Press, 2014.

Silverstein, Stuart. "Dodger Dogs Out at the Plate?" *Los Angeles Times*, 15 May 2007.

"The Size and Scope of the U.S. Hot Dog Market." *National Hot Dog and Sausage Council*. www.hot-dog.org

Skid, Nathan. "The Real Story Behind Detroit's Coney Wars." *Crain's Detroit Business*, 25 Jan. 2013.

"Slicing & Chopping Brisket." *The Virtual Weber Bullet*. www.virtualweberbullet.com

Smith, K. Annabelle. "The History of the Veggie Burger." *Smithsonian*. www.smithsonian.com

"SoDo." *Downtown Seattle*. www.downtownseattle.com

"Soft Shell Crab: Callinectes Sapidus." *Virginia Seafood*. www.virginiaseafood.org

"South Beach." *Visit Florida*. www.visitflorida.com

Stein, Fred. *A History of the Baseball Fan*. Jefferson, NC: McFarland, 2005.

Steinbach, Paul. "Concessions Contracts Capitalizing on Consumers' Brand Loyalty." *Athletic Business*. www.athleticbusiness.com

Stewart, Jennifer. "This Cheese-Stuffed, Bacon-Wrapped Corn Dog is 3000 Calories." *Business Week*, 16 Apr. 2014.

Stewart, Mark. "Minnie Minoso." *Society for American Baseball Research*. www.sabr.org

Stewart, Mark. "Orlando Cepeda." *Society for American Baseball Research*. www.sabr.org

Stone, Larry. "'Take Me Out to the Ball Game' Turns 100 Years Old." *Seattle Times*, 11 May 2008.

SOURCES

"Sweet Banana Pepper." *Bonnie Plants.* www.bonnieplants.com

Sylver, Adrienne. *Hot Diggity Dog: The History of the Hot Dog.* New York: Dutton Children's Books, 2010.

Taaffe, William. "The Sporting History of the Amazing Peanut." *Washington Star*, 3 Feb. 1977.

"Tad Dorgan." *New York Historical Society.* www.nyhistory.org

"Tad's Tid-Bits." *El Paso Herald*, 30 Dec. 1916 Home ed.

"Take Me Out to the Ball Game by Jack Norworth." *Baseball Almanac.* www.baseball-almanac.com

Tannenbaum, Kiri. "Snack Food Rewind: A History of Our Favorite Treats." *Delish.* www.delish.com

Taylor, Erica. "Little Known Black History Fact: Sweet Potato Pie." *blAck America Web.* blackamericaweb.com

"Texas Toast." *The Big Apple.* www.barrypopik.com

"Theodore Roosevelt: 1901-1909." *The White House.* www.whitehouse.gov

Thompson, Robert, Tim Wiles, and Andy Strasberg. *Baseball's Greatest Hit: The Story of Take Me Out to the Ball Game.* Milwaukee: Hal Leonard, 2008.

Thornley, Stew. *Holy Cow! The Life and Times of Halsey Hall.* Minneapolis: Nodin Press, 1991.

Thornley, Stew. *Land of the Giants: New York's Polo Grounds.* Philadelphia: Temple University Press, 2000.

"Todd Helton Biography." *JockBio.* www.jockbio.com

"Tommy Lasorda." *National Baseball Hall of Fame.* www.baseballhall.org

"Top 40 Orioles of All Time: #7, Boog Powell." *Camden Chat.* www.camdenchat.com

"Toronto's Spadina Ave. When It was a Quiet Rural Location." *Historic Toronto: Information on Toronto's History.* www.tayloronhistory.com

"Traverse Region." *Michigan Genealogy on the Web.* www.migenweb.org

"The Ultimate Cuban Sandwich Recipe." *Food Network.* www.foodnetwork.com

United States Department of Agriculture. *ChooseMyPlate.* www.choosemyplate.gov

"Vegetarianism in America." *Vegetarian Times.* www.vegetariantimes.com

"Veggie Dogs Go National at RFK." *Soy Happy.* www.soyhappy.org

"Vital Statistics: Jewish Population in the United States." *Jewish Virtual Library.* www.jewishvirtuallibrary.org

"Walleye." *Minnesota Department of Natural Resources.* www.dnr.state.mn.us

"Was Margherita Pizza Really Named After Italy's Queen?" *BBC.* www.bbc.co.uk

Weber, Roger. "A History of Food at the Ballpark." *Baseball Judgments.* baseballjudgments.tripod.com

Weinzweig, Ari. "Canadian Peameal Bacon." *Zingerman's Roadhouse.* www.zingermansroadhouse.com

"Welcome to Veggie Happy." *Veggie Happy.* www.veggiehappy.com

"What Are Rocky Mountain Oysters?" *WiseGEEK: Clear Answers for Common Questions.* www.wisegeek.org

"What Exactly is Pastrami?" *How Stuff Works.* www.howstuffworks.com

"What is Shawarma?" *WiseGEEK: Clear Answers for Common Questions.* www.wisegeek.org

"What is Tempeh?" *Tempeh.* www.tempeh.info

"What is the Difference Between a Hot Dog, Wiener, Frank, and Sausage?" *WiseGEEK: Clear Answers for Common Questions.* www.wisegeek.org

"What is the Difference Between Hot Dog and Sausage?" *Food Journey Singapore.* www.foodjourneysg.blogspot.com

"Willie Mays." *National Baseball Hall of Fame.* www.baseballhall.org

"Willie Stargell." *National Baseball Hall of Fame.* www.baseballhall.org

"Wise Foods Named Official Potato Chip and Cheez Doodle Sponsor for the New York Mets." *MLB.* www.mlb.com

Woo, Elaine. "Thomas G. Arthur, 84; Made Dodger Dogs a Staple of L.A. Stadium Experience."
Los Angeles Times, 27 Jun. 2006.

Wood, Bob. *Dodger Dogs to Fenway Franks: And All the Wieners In Between.* New York: McGraw-Hill, 1988.

Woods, Ashley. "Charley Marcuse, Detroit Tigers Singing Hot Dog Man, Possibly Fired for Anti-Ketchup Stance."
Huffington Post. www.huffingtonpost.com

"Yicketty." *Urban Dictionary.* www.urbandictionary.com

"Yogisms." *Washington Times.* www.washingtontimes.com

Zeimer, Gil. "Gordon Biersch Hits Home Run With Garlic Fries." *Intuit GoPayment.* www.blog.gopayment.com

Zeldes, Leah A. "'Tis the Seasonings: How Do Local Polish Butchers Elevate Sausage to an Art Form?"
Chicago Sun-Times, 22 Oct. 2008.

Zimmer, Erin. "What's a Half-Smoke?" *Serious Eats.* www.seriouseats.com